THE

Ultimate
Guide

TO

MUSIC

CARLTON KIDS

Joe Fullman

THIS IS A CARLTON BOOK

Text, design and illustration
© Carlton Books Limited 2014

Published in 2014 by
Carlton Books Limited
An imprint of the
Carlton Publishing Group
20 Mortimer Street,
London W1T 3JW

A catalogue record for this book is available from the British Library.

ISBN: 978-1-78312-091-8

Printed and bound in China

Executive Editor: Anna Brett
Editor: Joanna Pocock
Design Manager: Emily Clarke
Designer: Ceri Hurst
Picture Researcher: Steve Behan
Publisher: Russell McLean
Production: Marion Storz

Audio Acknowledgement:
The publishers would like to thank the Britten-Pears Foundation for their kind permission to use audio from a recording of *The Young Person's Guide to the Orchestra* performed by The Royal Northern College of Music Symphony Orchestra, conduced by Sir Mark Elder.

Picture Acknowledgements:
The publishers would like to thank the following sources for their kind permission to reproduce the pictures in this book.

Key: t=Top, b=Bottom, c=Centre, l=Left and r=Right.

1l Shutterstock.com, 1r. Doug Kanter/AFP/Getty Images, 2 & 6 Shutterstock.com, 7tl. D. Hunstein/Lebrecht Photo Library, 7tr Lebrecht Photo Library, 7c & 7bc Shutterstock. com, 8l & 8r Images courtesy of Fender Musical Instruments, 9b Courtesy of Roland Corporation, 10t Shutterstock.com, 10l Ray Mickshaw/FOX via Getty Images, 10c Yoshikazu Tsuno/AFP/Getty Images, 11bl 11tl Hiroyuki Ito/Getty Images, 11bc Joseph Okpako/Getty Images, 12t Bridgeman Images, 12c Christie Goodwin/Redferns via Getty Images, 13t David Goddard/Getty Images, 13tr Thinkstock, 13c Science Museum/Science & Society Picture Library, all rights reserved., 13b Simon Dawson/Bloomberg via Getty Images, 14l Carl Court/AFP/Getty Images, 14bl JP Jazz Archive/ Redferns, 15t FOX via Getty Images, 15c Amy Sussman/ Getty Images, 15b Michael Ochs Archives/Getty Images, 16c Chris Graythen/Getty Images, 16-17 Jack Vartoogian/Getty Images, 17tl Shutterstock.com, 17tr & 17cr Frank Driggs Collection/Getty Images, 17br Gilles Petard/Redferns/Getty Images, 18t EyeBrowz/Alamy, 18l Charles Trainor/Time & Life Pictures/Getty Images, 19c Digital Vision/Getty Images, 19cr Craig Lovell/Eagle Visions Photography/Alamy, 19br Gilles Petard/Redferns/Getty Images, 19bc Val Wilmer/ Redferns/Getty Images, 20t Rex Features/Richard Young, 20cl Jemal Countess/Getty Images, 20b Pictorial Press Ltd/ Alamy, 21t Rex Features/Ian Dickson, 21cr Rex Features/ Neil Stevenson, 21bc Suzi Pratt/FilmMagic/Getty Images, 22bl David Redfern/Redferns/Getty Images, 22c James Marshall/Corbis, 22r Tim Hall/Redferns/Getty Images, 22bc Jamie Squire/FIFA/FIFA via Getty Images, 23tl LightRocket via Getty Images, 23tr Christine Osborne/Corbis, 23bl Naho Yoshizawa/Aflo/Corbis, 24t & 24b Thinkstock, 24c Photo Resource Hawaii/Alamy, 25t Hemis/Alamy, 25c Antionio Scorza/AFP/Getty Images, 25b Shutterstock. com, 26c Images/Alamy, 26b Private Collection, 27c FOX via Getty Images, 27br Features/Everett Collection, 27bc Lucasfilm/20th Century Fox/The Kobal Collection/Connor, Frank, 28t Jacob Silberberg/Getty Images, 28l Topfoto. co.uk/The Granger Collection, 28c Private Collection, 28r

Akg-Images/Stefan Diller, 30t Popperfoto/Getty Images, 30c & 30cl Bridgeman Images, 30bc Bettmann/Corbis, 31tr Topical Press Agency/Getty Images, 31t & 31c Bridgeman Images, 31cr Colin Underhill/Alamy, 32t CBW/Alamy, 32l Time & Life Pictures/Getty Images, 32r Chris Morphet/ Redferns/Getty Images, 33t Michael Ochs Archives/Corbis, 33cl Keith Morris/Alamy, 33cr Ted Thai/Time & Life Pictures/ Getty Images, 34t Horizons WWP/Alamy, 34c Shutterstock. com, 34b Marc Tielemans/Alamy, 35t Rex Features, 35c Photononstop/Getty Images, 35b Rex Features/Edd Griffin, 36t Getty Images, 36bl Shutterstock.com, 36br Jonathan Alpeyrie/Getty Images, 37t Rex Features/Cultura, 37bc Shutterstock.com, 37c Jack Vartoogian/Getty Images, 38cl & 38bl Topfoto.co.uk/The Granger Collection, 38br Akg-Images/Erich Lessing, 39tc Topfoto.co.uk/Arena PAL, 39c Bridgeman Images, 39b China Photos/Getty Images, 40t The Art Archive/Alamy, 40c Bridgeman Images, 40b Private Collection, 41t Bridgeman Images, 41c Ivy Close Images/ Alamy, 41b Lebrecht Photo Library, 42l DeAgostini/Getty Images, 42r Hiroyuki Ito/Getty Images, 43t Hiroyuki Ito/ Getty Images, 43c DEA/A. Dagli Orti/De Agostini/Getty Images, 44l Bridgeman Images, 44r Bridgeman Images, 44t The Image Bank/Getty Images, 44cl Interfoto/Alamy, 44c Bridgeman Images, 44cr De Agostini/Getty Images, 45bl Hiroyuki Ito/Getty Images, 46c Bridgeman Images, 46b & 47t Shutterstock.com, 47c Leemage/UIG via Getty Images, 47cr Archive Photos/Getty Images, 48bl Bridgeman Images, 48bc Lebrecht Photo Library, 48br Rex Features/Snap, 49t & 49bc Lebrecht Photo Library, 49tc Hulton Archive/Getty Images, 49bc Stefan Simonsen/AFP/Getty Images, 50t Bridgeman Images, 50c Jo Hale/Getty Images, 50b Rex Features/ Alastair Muir, 51t Lebrecht Photo Library, 51c Shutterstock. com/Igor Bulgarin, 51c Rex Features/Thomas Bowles, 52t SuperStock/De Agostini, 52cr Bridgeman Images, 52bl John Kellerman/Alamy, 52bc & 53t Lebrecht Photo Library, 53bl Dieter Nagl/AFP/Getty Images, 53br DeAgostini/ Getty Images, 54cl Lebrecht Photo Library, 54cr & 54br Bridgeman Images, 55t CBS via Getty Images, 55c Yuri Kadobnov/AFP/Getty Images, 55b Linda Vartoogian/Getty Images, 56t & 56c Britten–Pears Foundation, 56b Bethany Clarke/Getty Images, 57t Hiroyuki Ito/Getty Images, 57c Hans Wild/Britten-Pears Foundation, 57b Matt Cardy/Getty Images, 58l Bridgeman Images, 59t & 59b Getty Images, 59c Hiroyuki Ito/Getty Images, 60t, 60l, 60cr, 60cl Shutterstock. com, 60cl Lebrecht Photo Library, 61 all Shutterstock.com

except 61tl & 61tr Getty Images, 62-63 Thinkstock.com, 63 Shutterstock.com, 63bl Stan Honda/AFP/Getty Images, 63br Iconica/Getty Images, 64cl Tim Graham/Getty Images, 64bl De Agostini Picture Library/Getty Images, 65l & 65r Getty Images, 66bc Lebrecht Photo Library, 66br, 67bl, Courtesy of Fender Musical Instruments Corporation, 67tl Shutterstock.com, 68t Lebrecht Photo Library, 68cl, 68c, 68b Shutterstock.com, 69 all Shutterstock.com except 69cl, 69c Thinkstock.com, 70-71 Shutterstock.com, 70 DK/Alamy, 71c Getty Images, 71r Courtesy of Brookhaven National Lab, 72-73 Shutterstock.com, 72bl Press Association Images/DPA, 72t Lebrecht Music and Arts Photo Library/ Alamy, 73tr YAY Media/Alamy AS, 73cr Selmer.fr, 74c Getty Images, 74l Shutterstock.com, 74t Private Collection, 75 all Shutterstock except 75cr Private Collection and 75br Getty Images, 76-77 Shutterstock.com, 76t Private Collection, 77tr Prashanth Vishwanathan/Bloomberg via Getty Images, 77bc Photographer's Choice/Getty Images, 77br AWL Images/Getty Images, 78-79 & 79 Shutterstock.com, 78bl Lebrecht Photo Library, 79tr Erik Sampers/Gamma-Rapho via Getty Images, 79br & 80t Lebrecht Photo Library, 80 all Shutterstock.com, 81 all Shutterstock.com except (gong, glockenspiel, chimes & claves) Getty Images, (wooden block) LP Aspire, (tambourine) Thinkstock.com, (whip) Private Collection, 82bl Nigel Osbourne/Redferns/Getty Images, 82br & 83t © Courtesy of Pearl Drums, 83br David Redfern/Redferns/Getty Images, 84t Directphoto Collection/ Alamy, 84c DK/Getty Images, 84b Shutterstock.com, 85 (upright piano, pipe organ) Shutterstock.com, 85 (Ondes Martenot) Lebrecht Music and Arts Photo Library/Alamy, 85 (clavichord, harmonium & electric organ) Getty Images, 85 (keyboard synth) Thinkstock.com, 86c & 86cr Lebrecht Photo Library, 86bl Craig Warga/Bloomberg via Getty Images, 87t Shutterstock.com, 87br DK/Getty Images, 88bl sydneymedia.com.au, 88tc Getty Images, 88c Jo Miyake/ Alamy, 88t & 88b Thinkstock.com, 90c, 90bc & 91tr Lebrecht Photo Library, 90bl Hiroyuki Ito/Getty Images, 92t © Clive Strutt, 92bl DeAgostini/Getty Images.

Every effort has been made to acknowledge correctly and contact the source and/or copyright holder of each picture and Carlton Books Limited apologises for any unintentional errors or omissions, which will be corrected in future editions of this book.

CONTENTS

The sections of this book are colour-coded, see below for detail on what these chapters contain.

HOW TO USE YOUR
FREE APP

HOW DOES IT WORK?

Your app uses Augmented Reality (AR) which mixes the real and the virtual worlds together, so that a mobile device with a camera can bring books to life with amazing interactive animations.

WHAT DO I NEED?

To run the Augmented Reality animations, all you need is this book and a device that meets the minimum system requirements (see below).

HOW TO USE AR

It's easy! Here's what you have to do...

1 Download the free MusicGuide iOS App from the Apple App Store or the MusicGuide Android App from Google Play.

2 Launch the MusicGuide App to open the home page. Tap one of the three experience buttons to begin.

3 Hold your mobile device up to pages 92–93 to start your interactive audio experience and make sure the volume is turned up.

WHAT YOUR APP CONTAINS

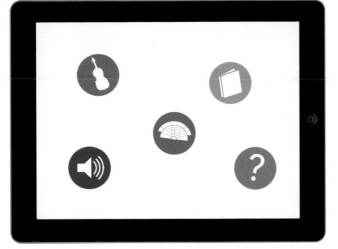

Your home screen allows you to access three different interactive experiences as well as help and a link to buy the book.

Experience one allows you to view the instruments of the orchestra, zoom in and out and listen to them play.

Experience two requires you to drag and drop the instruments into the correct sections of the orchestra. There's an audio reward if you get it right!

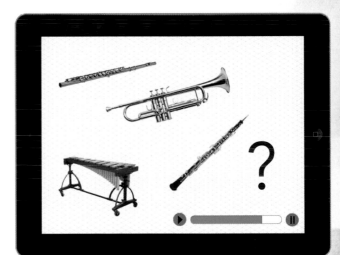

Experience three puts your knowledge to the test as you have to identify the instrument from an audio clip. Can you complete all the levels?

System Requirements
Apple devices using iOS version 5.1 and above, including iPhone 4S and above; iPod 5 Gen; iPad 2 and above; plus compatible Android devices using Android version 2.3 and above, OpenGL version 2.0. All devices need both front and rear facing cameras.

NEED SOME HELP?

If you've got a problem, check out our website:
www.carltonbooks.co.uk/ music/help

WHAT IS MUSIC?

PUT SIMPLY, MUSIC IS THE PLEASING ARRANGEMENT OF NOTES. But what makes them pleasing can be difficult to define. Every culture produces its own forms of music, which may seem to have little in common with each other. And there are many different reasons for making music – it can be made for its own sake, for religious reasons, or to accompany another art form, such as a film. But, at a basic level, all music works in the same way and uses the same key elements. The main ones are **pitch**, **melody** and **rhythm**.

SOUND WAVES

We experience music in the same way that we hear all noise: as **sound waves**. A sound wave is the movement of air caused when something vibrates – such as a musical instrument or the speaker in a stereo. The vibration of the object vibrates the air particles next to it, which pass the vibration on to the particles next to them, and so on. Our ears detect this movement as sound.

ABOVE LEFT: The string of a guitar vibrates to create sound.

LEFT: Different types of wave produce different sounds. The higher the peak of the wave, the louder the note.

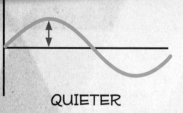

QUIETER

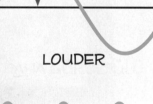

LOUDER

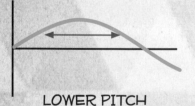

LOWER PITCH

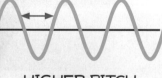

HIGHER PITCH

PITCH AND FREQUENCIES

The pitch of a note is how high or low it sounds. This is determined by the **frequency** of the sound wave – the number of times it vibrates per second. The higher the frequency, the higher the note. The frequency of a sound wave can be shown as a wavy line – the closer together the peaks of the line are, the higher the frequency.

DID YOU KNOW?

Humans can only hear sounds between a certain range of frequencies, typically between 20 Hz (very low) to 20,000 Hz (very high). Many animals, such as dogs, can hear frequencies that are much higher.

GROUPING NOTES

Notes are divided into groups called **scales**. A lot of **Western** music is based on the **chromatic scale**, which consists of 12 notes, in a sequence of **semitones**. On a keyboard, these notes are arranged in repeating patterns of seven white notes and five black notes. This pattern is known as an **octave** – from the Latin for 'eighth' because the pattern repeats after every seventh whole tone.

BELOW: An octave on a keyboard.

Symphonie № 5.

RIGHT: The score for the famous opening theme of Beethoven's *Fifth Symphony.*

ABOVE: A pianist playing chords.

MELODY

The melody is the bit you sing along to. Most Western music is based on melody – single notes that have been arranged to form patterns, or tunes. In classical music, a piece may have several melodies, including a main melody, or theme, as well as a number of variations of this theme. Popular music and folk music typically have fewer melodies – perhaps just a verse and chorus. Jazz musicians **improvise** new melodies using the chord sequence of an existing tune.

LEFT: A drummer keeps the rhythm steady.

HARMONY

Harmony is the combination of two or more notes. A **chord** is formed when at least three notes are played together. Much Western music – including classical, popular and jazz – is based on melody lines that are sung or played over sequences of chords (known as chord progressions). Melody has been around since ancient times. But harmony didn't become a major part of Western music until around 1600 (see pages 42–43).

RHYTHM

The rhythm is the feel or pulse of the music – the bit that makes you tap your foot or nod your head. It's a combination of several musical elements, including the **tempo** of the music, the time value of each note, the rests between the notes, and the pattern of **beats** as shown by the **time signature**.

WHAT ARE INSTRUMENTS?

MOST MUSIC IS MADE USING INSTRUMENTS.
There are two principal types: percussion instruments, which can be hit or shaken to make a rhythm; and melodic instruments, which play the notes. Percussion and melodic instruments can be further divided into three main categories: **acoustic**, **electric** and **electronic**. This depends on whether the sound is made by the instrument itself (acoustic) or by some form of technology (electric and electronic).

ACOUSTIC INSTRUMENTS

When a musician plays an acoustic instrument, such as a violin or a flute, the sound is **amplified** solely by the instrument. Traditionally, most classical music is created using acoustic instruments. The main types of instrument making up a classical orchestra are stringed instruments, wind instruments, brass instruments, percussion instruments and keyboard instruments.

ELECTRIC INSTRUMENTS

When a musician plays an electric instrument, such as an electric violin, the sound is amplified using the instrument's technology. Many electric instruments are based on acoustic instruments. For instance, the electric guitar is an adaptation of the acoustic guitar. Instead of using the instrument's body to project the sound of the strings' vibrations, it converts these vibrations into an electric signal, which can then be greatly amplified.

RIGHT: An electric guitar with a solid body and pickups that turn the sound into an electrical signal.

PICKUPS

ABOVE: An acoustic guitar with a hollow body that resonates the sound.

ELECTRONIC INSTRUMENTS

When a musician plays an electronic instrument, such as a synthesizer, the sound is both created and amplified by the instrument. The first electronic instruments were produced in the 1920s. These included the theremin, which has two antennae that sense the movements of a musician's hands in the air to produce eerie, swooping sounds.

ABOVE: Leon Theremin playing the electronic instrument he invented in the 1920s.

SAMPLERS

Samplers are like synthesizers, but instead of generating their own sounds, they record (or **sample**) other sounds, usually from existing recordings. These samples can then be mixed with other samples to create new pieces of music. Samples can also be adapted – for instance their pitch can be raised or lowered, or their tempo speeded up or slowed down – to create new effects.

BELOW: A sampler that can be used for recording and adapting music.

SYNTHESIZERS

The synthesizer is one of the best-known electronic instruments and can be used to create a wide variety of sounds. These include sounds that imitate (or 'synthesize') existing instruments, such as a piano or a violin, and non-musical sounds, such as bird song or a helicopter (which can then be played at different pitches). It can also create new sounds that don't exist in nature. Most synthesizers are played using a keyboard, though there are also guitar synthesizers, wind synthesizers and electronic drum kits.

ABOVE: The jazz musician Herbie Hancock plays a portable synthesizer called a 'keytar'.

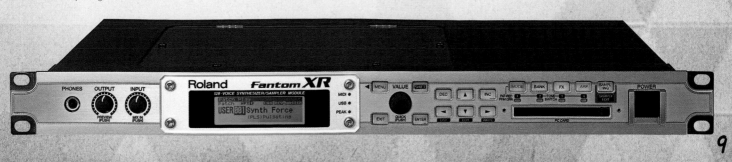

WHAT ARE VOCALS?

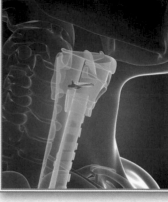

THERE IS ONE INSTRUMENT THAT IS COMMON TO ALL COUNTRIES AND CULTURES – THE HUMAN VOICE. From the earliest times to today, the best-loved music often features singing. The voice is an extremely versatile instrument, capable of tackling a wide range of notes and conveying intense emotions. A singer can perform on their own or accompanied by instruments, as a soloist or alongside other singers in a choir.

HOW WE SING

The human voice works a bit like a wind instrument, with air passing through a tube – in this case the windpipe (trachea) – to make sound. At the top of the windpipe is the voice box (larynx), which has two pieces of membrane called vocal cords stretched across it. When we speak or sing, they are pulled tight and the air passing over them from our lungs causes them to vibrate, creating sound.

ABOVE: Singers performing on a TV talent show.

RIGHT: The voices of these opera singers range from very low (bass) to very high (soprano).

SINGING IN TUNE

We don't just sing with our mouths. Our ears are equally important, as they help us to detect the right notes. The brain can then direct our throat and mouth to form the shapes that let us sing the notes correctly. Some people are better at hearing and replicating pitches than others, which is why some people can sing in tune, while others can't – as TV talent programmes show.

VOCAL RANGES

Everyone has a natural range of notes they can sing. Some people have low, booming voices, while others can sing high, piercing notes. Generally, children and women have a higher singing range than men. All human voices fall into one of the four main ranges in classical music composition. These are, from highest to lowest: soprano, alto, tenor and bass.

LEFT: Singers perform *Messiah*, an 18th-century choral work by George Frideric Handel (1685–1759).

SINGING TOGETHER

Music performed by large groups of vocalists, either with or without instruments, is known as choral music. Unaccompanied singing is called 'a cappella'. Choral music usually involves harmony – singing different notes at the same time. Choirs most commonly sing four-part harmonies, although five-, six- and eight-part harmonies are also known. Some of the greatest classical composers, including Handel and Beethoven, wrote choral music.

SUGGESTED LISTENING

A CAPPELLA: Pentatonix
Evolution of Music

HIGH NOTES: Mariah Carey *Emotions*

LOW NOTES: Paul Robeson
Ol' Man River from Showboat

CHORAL: Carl Orff
O Fortuna from Carmina Burana

DIFFERENT SINGING STYLES

Across the world, there are many cultural differences in the way people sing. For instance, in Chinese or Peking opera, a high, nasal style of singing is used, whereas in Western operas, performers have developed ways of powerfully projecting their voices, so they can be heard over the music. Modern popular singers rely on microphones for amplification, which means they can sing quietly and still be heard. Rappers talk or chant over the top of the music.

ABOVE: A singer with the China National Peking Opera Company.

LEFT: The rapper Jay Z performing with a microphone.

DID YOU KNOW?

The throat-singing people of Tuva, Russia, can manipulate their voices so that they can sing two (and sometimes more) notes at the same time.

EXPERIENCING
MUSIC

A CENTURY AGO, A LIVE PERFORMANCE WAS THE ONLY WAY MOST PEOPLE COULD ENJOY MUSIC.
Today, thanks to technological developments – including the invention of recording, electrical amplification and the internet – music is everywhere. It's on the radio and TV, on the soundtrack to films and piped into shops. Every year, millions of records are sold in stores or downloaded online, and countless concerts and festivals are held around the world. People even carry around personal stereos, so they can listen to music whenever and wherever they want.

ABOVE: An illustration of a church choir in Venice, 1512.

CHURCH MUSIC

Music plays an important role in most religions. In Europe and the Americas, the Christian church was one of the main places people went to experience music – in the form of hymns and carols – before the invention of recorded music in the 19th century. Church music in the Middle Ages – particularly the **plainchant** performed in monasteries – was a major influence on the development of classical music.

ABOVE: Fans attend a live concert by the pop singer Katy Perry in 2013.

PUBLIC CONCERTS

In the Middle Ages, people in Europe heard music in church or when groups of travelling musicians – called minstrels – came to town. Over time, popular music (music performed for enjoyment rather than worship) became more widespread. The first theatres for musical performances were built in the 17th century, and their number increased greatly over the next few centuries. Today, music is staged everywhere from small venues to enormous sports stadiums where pop acts put on spectacular shows.

DID YOU KNOW?

The biggest concert ever staged saw 3.5 million people gather on a beach in Rio de Janeiro to hear the British singer, Rod Stewart, perform in 1994.

FESTIVALS

The improvement of amplification technology in the 20th century allowed concerts to become bigger and louder than ever before. Multi-day music festivals, where popular musicians play to hundreds of thousands of people, have become popular since the 1960s. Britain's Glastonbury Festival attracts more than 175,000 people over five days. It is Europe's largest music festival.

ABOVE: Radio sets, such as this one from the 1920s, helped popularize music.

RECORDED MUSIC

Perhaps no development has helped the spread of music more than the invention of recording in the late 19th century (see pages 30–31). For the first time, people could experience music in their own homes. Today, recorded music is one of the world's biggest entertainment industries with millions of records sold each year. People can listen to music using many different devices, from large hi-fi systems to portable personal stereos.

RADIO

In the early 20th century, scientists found ways to send information through the air via radio waves. This led to the development of radio (in the 1920s) and TV (in the 1930s). These two technologies greatly increased the amount of music that people could enjoy. Many radio stations are dedicated solely to playing music, while TV programmes help to turn musicians into celebrities recognized the world over.

THE INTERNET

The invention of the World Wide Web in 1989 had almost as great an impact on how people experienced music as the introduction of recording around a century earlier. Millions of songs are now available to download, stream or watch online at the touch of a button.

LEFT: A computer screen showing music by The Beatles available to download.

TYPES OF MUSIC

THERE ARE HUNDREDS OF DIFFERENT TYPES OF MUSIC, BUT ALL MUSIC FITS INTO JUST A FEW BROAD CATEGORIES.
The main ones are classical, jazz, popular music, world music and folk music. The first three refer mainly to the music of the Western world. Classical and jazz are both seen as 'serious' forms where skilled musicians write and play complicated pieces. Popular music, on the other hand, is regarded as 'simple', catchy music created to entertain people. World music is a general term used to describe music from outside the Western world.

CLASSICAL MUSIC

Classical music is difficult to define. Many people think of it as music played by large orchestras, but it can also be played by small groups. It's sometimes considered old music, but there's plenty of modern classical too. Above all, it forms part of a tradition of composition, performance and **musical notation** stretching back to the Middle Ages. Scholars divide the history of music into six periods: Medieval, Renaissance, Baroque, Classical, Romantic and 20th century (see pages 40–49).

ABOVE LEFT: A 2013 performance at the BBC Proms – a popular annual festival of classical music in the UK.

DID YOU KNOW?

Leif Segerstam (b. 1944) from Finland has written more **symphonies** than any other composer – in excess of 280.

JAZZ

There are many different types of jazz: trad jazz, cool jazz, free jazz and more. Although they can sound very different from one another, they all grew out of a type of music that emerged in the southern United States around 1900. The music was a mixture of African rhythms and European harmonies and melodies. What unites all jazz styles is improvisation, with musicians making up solos based around set patterns (see page 16).

LEFT: The jazz saxophonist John Coltrane performs with his band in 1961.

ABOVE: The popular band One Direction in 2013.

POPULAR MUSIC

Popular music is created more as entertainment than art. It usually takes the form of songs or short instrumental pieces sold individually as **singles** or **albums**. With catchy melodies and rhythms, popular songs are designed to be instantly appealing. Since the emergence of rock and roll in the 1950s and the growth of the recorded music industry, popular music has become one of the world's most successful and influential forms of culture (see pages 18–21).

RIGHT: The South African male choral group Ladysmith Black Mambazo.

WORLD MUSIC

Most of the music featured in this book is part of the 'Western tradition' – music from Europe and the United States that uses similar scales and musical techniques. But the music of Africa, Asia, South America and elsewhere has very different traditions and rules. Musicians in these places often use scales and rhythms that can sound strange to Western ears. Any music produced outside the Western tradition can be referred to as world music (see pages 22–25).

SUGGESTED LISTENING

CLASSICAL: Beethoven Fifth Symphony

JAZZ: Duke Ellington Take the 'A' Train

POP: The Beatles She Loves You

WORLD MUSIC: Rachid Taha Ya Rayah

FOLK MUSIC: Woody Guthrie This Land is Your Land

FOLK AND TRADITIONAL MUSIC

Classical music is traditionally enjoyed by those at the top of society. Folk music is the music of local communities at the other end of the social spectrum. It's not supposed to be art, like classical music, or entertainment, like popular music. Instead, it usually relates the stories, history and beliefs of these communities and may contain political messages. Throughout history, folk music was often not written down, but was passed **orally** from one generation to the next.

LEFT: The US folk singer Woody Guthrie in the early 1940s.

JAZZ

SUGGESTED LISTENING

JAZZ IS A FORM OF MUSIC THAT EMERGED IN THE UNITED STATES AROUND 1900.

A mixture of African American and European musical traditions, it featured complex rhythms and intricate melodies. Over the next few decades, this new music became hugely popular and many different styles of jazz evolved. Jazz can be played on any instruments, but some of the most common ones are drums, double bass, piano, saxophone and trumpet. Jazz music is usually partly improvised.

Scott Joplin *Maple Leaf Rag*
Louis Armstrong *Potato Head Blues*
Charlie Parker *Ornithology*
Dave Brubeck *Take 5*

INVENTING JAZZ

Jazz was born in the bars of New Orleans, a music-loving city in the southern United States. Here communities from Africa, Europe, South America and the Caribbean met and shared musical influences. Jazz was a combination of many different elements, including African rhythms, European scales and harmonies, and call and response songs originally sung by people working in the fields.

LEFT: The Preservation Hall Jazz Band play on Bourbon Street in New Orleans in 2006.

A typical jazz band featuring piano, saxophone, double bass, trumpet and drums.

PLAYING JAZZ

Jazz musicians don't perform songs exactly as they're written, but improvise – or make up – melodies based on set themes. The rhythm section – typically the drums and **bass** instruments – sets the tempo and plays the chords, while the lead instruments, such as the saxophone and trumpet, take turns improvising solos. This means that no two jazz performances are exactly the same.

THE SAXOPHONE

The saxophone is one of the most popular jazz instruments, often used for soloing. Adolphe Sax, who invented (and gave his name to) the instrument in 1840, intended it to be a cross between a wind instrument and a brass instrument. It's played with a mouthpiece and has similar fingering to a clarinet, but it's much more powerful with a wide bell for projecting the sound, like a trumpet.

RIGHT: The saxophone is a wind instrument made of brass.

DID YOU KNOW?

Not all improvisation is done by instruments. Jazz singers often perform improvised sections with made-up words and tunes known as 'scatting'. Ella Fitzgerald was one of the most famous scat singers.

RAGTIME

Military marches were very popular in the United States in the 1800s. Around 1900, musicians such as Scott Joplin began adapting and modernizing these songs. They changed the rigid, marching rhythms to looser, African-style beats creating a jaunty, danceable style of music. This new style became known as ragtime because of its jerky, 'ragged' rhythm.

ABOVE: Sheet music cover for a Scott Joplin song.

BIG BAND

In the 1920s, a new style of jazz appeared that was loud, lively and meant to be danced to. Played by large groups of musicians (around 17–25 people) and featuring rhythm, brass, woodwind sections and often a singer – it became known as 'big band' music. It was also called 'swing' music because the tunes seemed to bounce along. By the 1930s, it had become the most popular music of the era.

ABOVE: Louis Armstrong and his famous All Stars.

BEBOP

In the 1940s, jazz musicians began to experiment, playing fast, complex harmonies, unusual melodies and unpredictable rhythms. This became known as 'bebop' after the noise of a honking saxophone. Some people didn't like the new, difficult music and the jazz world divided into two camps: the traditionalists who favoured conventional music and the modernists who wanted more experimentation.

ABOVE: Charlie Parker plays 'bebop' in 1948.

POPULAR MUSIC

THE ROCK AND ROLL ERA

FOR AS LONG AS THERE HAS BEEN SERIOUS ARTISTIC OR RELIGIOUS MUSIC, THERE HAS BEEN POPULAR MUSIC MADE FOR PEOPLE TO ENJOY.

Before the invention of recorded music, songs became well known through public performances and sales of sheet music. But in the mid-20th century, Western popular music became a global phenomenon following the arrival of an exciting new musical form in the United States: rock and roll. This was a mixture of many existing styles from both African American communities (including blues, gospel and rhythm and blues), and white communities (country and western music).

DID YOU KNOW?

The 1954 song 'Rock Around the Clock' is the most successful rock and roll song of all time, having sold more than 25 million copies. Its success helped kickstart the rock and roll era.

THE BIRTH OF ROCK AND ROLL

In the early 1950s, new technologies improved the quality of sound recordings and introduced new formats for listening to music – **vinyl** singles and albums. These helped to popularize rock and roll, a new, fast, beat-heavy music designed for dancing. It was particularly well liked by teenagers, a new social group that hadn't really existed before this time – but which would be hugely influential in the growth of popular music.

LEFT: The world's biggest-selling rock and roll singer, Elvis Presley, in 1956.

BLUES

Blues, which originated in the southern United States around 1900, is both a style of music and a form of musical composition. All blues songs use a repeated pattern of chords. But not all blues songs sound the same. Early blues music was sparse and simple, often performed by a singer with an acoustic guitar. More complex styles, using electric guitars and full bands, developed later in the 20th century. Blues songs are often about sad subjects – to 'have the blues' means to 'be sad'.

ABOVE: John Lee Hooker playing the blues in 1992.

GOSPEL

A type of Christian religious music often performed by choirs, gospel can trace its roots back to the African American churches of the late 19th century. Unlike many traditional forms of church music, such as hymns, which tend be slow-paced with a steady rhythm, gospel is lively with a fast-paced, **syncopated** rhythm. Gospel music is still very popular in the United States.

RIGHT: Gospel singers, with raised hands, sing in a church service.

COUNTRY MUSIC

Country music, also called country and western music, began as a type of folk music played by local white communities in the rural southern United States. It usually took the form of dance numbers or slow **ballads** played on string instruments, such as banjos, guitars and violins. From the 1950s onwards, country music became popular across the United States, although it didn't enjoy the same level of international success as rock and roll.

BELOW: The country band Cow Bop in 2011.

SUGGESTED LISTENING

ROCK AND ROLL:
Little Richard Tutti Frutti

BLUES: Robert Johnson Crossroads

GOSPEL: Edwin Hawkins Singers
Oh Happy Day

RHYTHM AND BLUES: Ray Charles
What'd I Say

SOUL: Aretha Franklin
A Natural Woman

LEFT: The R&B singer Ray Charles in 1959.

R&B

A major influence on rock and roll, rhythm and blues (or R&B) was itself influenced by several other musical styles, including blues, gospel and jazz. It was an energetic, lively music with strong danceable rhythms. Popular in America's black communities from the 1940s onwards, its later adoption by white singers and audiences helped fuel the rock and roll explosion.

LEFT: Aretha Franklin, the 'Queen of Soul' in the mid-1960s.

SOUL

Soul emerged in the early rock and roll era as a mixture of R&B and gospel. Soul songs are often very emotional and 'soulful', which is how the music got its name. Early on, soul was mainly performed by African Americans. But it crossed over to enjoy enormous mainstream success in the 1960s.

POPULAR MUSIC
THE 1950s TO TODAY

ROCK AND ROLL WASN'T JUST A NEW TYPE OF MUSIC, IT CHANGED THE WAY WE LISTEN TO MUSIC. Its popularity fuelled the sale of vinyl singles and albums – introduced just a few years before – turning recorded music into a huge industry and popular musicians into global stars. It also had a major influence on the development of society – particularly in fashion and social attitudes. Many different styles of popular music emerged following the birth of rock and roll in the early 1950s. These pages look at some of the most successful.

ABOVE: Rock band U2 performs in London in 20...

POP

'Pop' is the abbreviation for popular music, but it doesn't mean exactly the same thing. Popular music is any style of music designed to have mainstream appeal. Pop is a specific type of popular music, consisting of relatively short songs, based around catchy **hooks** and **choruses**, which generally have a light-hearted feel. Most of the music in the singles chart could be described as 'pop'.

ABOVE: Lady Gaga performs her pop act in 2011.

ROCK

Rock emerged in the 1960s as a more serious alternative to pop. Rock musicians tend to play longer songs than pop artists and place greater emphasis on musicianship. The typical rock band consists of a singer, an electric guitarist, a bass guitarist, a keyboard player and a drummer. Rock bands, such as The Beatles, helped to popularize the idea of an album being a work of art rather than just a collection of songs.

PUNK

Punk was a reaction to the long, complex, largely instrumental rock songs that were popular in the early 1970s. Punk musicians favoured short, loud songs that often had a political message. Like many musical genres, punk musicians (and their fans) had a distinct look characterized by spiky hair, ripped clothing and thick make-up.

LEFT: The punk singer Johnny Rotten on stage in 1977.

FUNK AND DISCO

Funk came out of soul and jazz in the late 1960s, and emphasizes rhythm over melody. It often features simple chord progressions using electric guitar, bass guitar, electric organ and brass instruments to create a rhythm or 'groove'. It is related to disco, which became popular in the late 1970s. Disco uses a strong, repetitive beat known as 'four-to-the-floor'. Both funk and disco are forms of dance music.

REGGAE

RIGHT: Bob Marley, who made reggae international.

Made famous by singers such as Bob Marley, reggae was one of the first musical styles not from the US or the UK to achieve worldwide popularity. Originating in Jamaica, it was a combination of Caribbean styles (including calypso, mento and ska) and US influences (particularly R&B and jazz). Reggae has a steady, chopping rhythm made by the guitar (and sometimes the keyboard instruments) playing short, single chords on the **offbeat** of every bar.

RAP AND HIP HOP

Rap rewrote the rules of popular music in the 1970s and 80s. Traditionally, songs took the form of a vocalist singing a melody over instrumental music. But DJs in the US began to rap – chant rhyming verses – over existing records, or to repeat sections of records known as 'samples'. It soon became hugely popular, growing into an entire culture encompassing music, dancing (particularly break dancing) and art (in the form of graffiti).

SUGGESTED LISTENING

POP: Madonna Holiday

ROCK: The Rolling Stones Jumpin' Jack Flash

PUNK: The Clash London Calling

FUNK: James Brown Papa's Got a Brand New Bag

DISCO: Chic Good Times

REGGAE: Bob Marley Could You Be Loved

RAP: Sugarhill Gang Rapper's Delight

ELECTRONIC DANCE: Candi Staton You've Got the Love

RIGHT: People dance to electronic music.

ABOVE: The rapper Snoop Dogg performs live in 2013.

LEFT: A woman disco dances in the late 1970s.

ELECTRONIC DANCE MUSIC

In the mid-1970s, new electronic instruments, such as synthesizers, drum machines and samplers, became available that produced strange new sounds. Easy to play, they could be used by non-instrumentalists to make music. In the 1980s and 90s, new types of dance music emerged, including house, techno and garage, often featuring samples, synthesizer-generated bass lines and precise beats made on drum machines.

WORLD MUSIC

THE TERM 'WORLD MUSIC' IS USED TO DESCRIBE A VAST RANGE OF MUSICAL STYLES FROM ALL ACROSS THE GLOBE.
The songs of South America, Africa and Asia may have little in common with one another, but they are all forms of world music. World music reflects the cultures and traditions of the people who make it, often using very different scales and rhythms to the Western styles of European and North American music. These next four pages look at some of the most popular types of world music.

AFRICA

PERCUSSION

Percussion plays a big part in the music of Africa. Musicians use shakers, rattles and gongs, as well as many types of drum. One of the most popular drums is the West African djembe, made from a carved log covered in goatskin and played with the hands. African music uses different rhythms to Western music, and they can often be very complex.

LEFT: Fela Kuti plays the saxophone in 1987.

RIGHT: A djembe drum.

SOUTH AFRICA

For 60 years, the musicians of South Africa have been mixing traditional African music with Western popular music to create new styles. These have included Pennywhistle Jive in the 1950s, a dance style featuring an instrument used in cattle herding, and Bubblegum in the 1980s, a pop style using vocals and synthesizers. Kwaito, the country's version of hip hop, emerged in the 2000s, with rhymes chanted over **looped** samples.

AFROBEAT

In recent decades, African music has absorbed many Western influences resulting in new styles. Afrobeat was the 1970s creation of the Nigerian musician Fela Kuti. He combined the traditional Yoruba drumming and chanted vocals of his home country with US styles such as jazz and funk, and the new style became very popular in Africa and beyond.

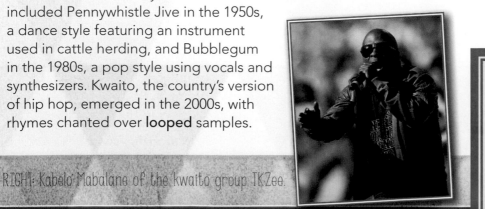

DID YOU KNOW?

The djembe is said to consist of three spirits: the spirit of the tree from which it was made, the spirit of the animal whose skin covers the head, and the spirit of the drum maker.

RIGHT: Kabelo Mabalane of the kwaito group TKZee.

ABOVE: Musicians perform in a gamelan orchestra in Bali, Indonesia.

CHINA

ABOVE: A scene from a Chinese opera.

As the world's oldest continuous civilization, China has been making music for thousands of years. But with more than a billion people and over 50 ethnic groups, China doesn't have one type of music. Every region has its own traditions, instruments and styles. One of the most well known forms of Chinese music is Chinese (or Peking) opera, a mixture of music, drama and dancing usually performed in elaborate costumes.

JAPAN

The koto is the national instrument of Japan, and koto music is an important part of traditional Japanese culture. About 180 cm (71 in) long with 13 (or more) strings stretched tight over a wooden frame, the koto is played by pressing down the strings with one hand and plucking with the other. Each string sits on a movable bridge, which can be shifted to change the string's pitch.

LEFT: A woman in a traditional Japanese kimono plays the koto.

INDONESIA

The traditional 'gamelan' orchestras of Indonesia consist of percussion instruments, such as drums and gongs – the word 'gamelan' means 'to hammer'. Some also feature wooden flutes and metallophones, which are a bit like xylophones with metal bars that are struck with mallets. No two gamelan orchestras have exactly the same instruments. Gamelan music is played at theatre performances and religious festivals.

INDIA

Indian music is not usually written down. Instead, musicians learn how to play by imitating other players. A typical piece of Indian music is made up of a rag (melody), a tal (rhythm) and a drone (a single, sustained note played throughout a piece). The musicians improvise – or make up – the music based on certain patterns of notes. One of the main instruments is the sitar, which is long-necked with six or seven main strings that are plucked with a metal pick. It produces a shimmering, quavering sound.

LEFT: An Indian sitar.

THE MIDDLE EAST

ARABIC MUSIC

The musical styles of the Arabic-speaking countries of the Middle East and North Africa share many characteristics. They are mainly vocal and use a lot of improvisation. Songs use scales that are very different to those used in the West. Traditional instruments include the rabab (a small violin-like instrument) and the oud (or lute), as well as Western instruments including electric guitars and violins. Harmony is not common in Arabic music.

ABOVE: A Middle Eastern oud.

THE PACIFIC

POLYNESIA

Polynesia is a collection of islands spread out across the Pacific Ocean. The people here developed a simple chant-based music and a form of dance which interprets the songs using hand gestures and hip movements. The Hawaiian hula is the most famous example of this dance. Polynesian music was greatly influenced by hymns brought over by Christian missionaries from the United States and Europe in the 19th century.

LEFT: Hula dancers perform wearing grass skirts and flower necklaces called leis.

AUSTRALIA

The first people reached Australia around 40,000 years ago. They developed their own music, isolated from the rest of the world until European settlers arrived in the late 18th century. This music is an important part of the Aboriginal people's culture, passed down the generations along with their stories. It uses mainly voices and instruments including the bilma (clapstick) and a long, low wind instrument called a yidaki (didgeridoo).

BELOW: A hand-carved didgeridoo.

DID YOU KNOW?

According to Aboriginal beliefs, Australia is crossed by paths known as songlines. Their routes can be retold as songs, which the Aborigines can use to find their way around.

ISLAND MUSIC

The Caribbean-island chain has been the source of some of the most internationally successful world music, including reggae from Jamaica, calypso and steel band music from Trinidad and merengue from the Dominican Republic. The population is mainly made up of the descendants of African slaves and European settlers, and the music is a mixture of their influences. Each island has its own style, but they are all highly melodic with syncopated rhythms and an emphasis on offbeats.

LEFT: A girl plays a steel drum during carnival in Trinidad.

THE AMERICAS

NATIVE AMERICAN MUSIC

Many of the world's most popular forms of music have come out of the Americas. A good deal of these have been been created by the immigrant populations that arrived after 1500. But Native Americans also have their own music. In North America this mainly takes the form of singing with simple percussion instruments, such as drums and rattles. Native South American music features a greater range of instruments, including clay and wooden pipes.

BELOW: Panpipe players performing at a carnival in Bolivia.

ABOVE: A percussionist sings and dances in Brazil's famous carnival in Rio de Janeiro.

BRAZIL

The music of Brazil has been influenced by many different peoples, including its indigenous inhabitants, Portuguese colonists and African slaves. Today, one of its most popular musical forms is samba, a high-tempo music played on a mixture of drums, percussion and stringed instruments, which is based on a traditional African dance. Samba is the sound of the world's biggest carnival, held in Rio de Janeiro, when samba groups dance through the streets dressed in colourful costumes.

MUSIC FOR
FILM AND TV

MUSIC ISN'T ALWAYS CREATED PURELY FOR ITS OWN SAKE. Sometimes it's used to accompany other art forms, such as a film or a TV show. Composers of movie themes and soundtracks have to make sure their music fits in with the tone of the story being told. If the story is sad or happy or exciting, then the music needs to convey those feelings to the audience. It should also match the action as closely as possible.

EARLY FILM MUSIC

For the first few decades of the film industry, in the early 1900s, movies didn't have sound. Words were sometimes displayed on screen to explain what a character was doing, and there would often be a pianist, organist or even a whole orchestra in the cinema, playing along with the movie. They'd try to match the music to the pictures, playing fast during a chase scene or slow and tenderly during a romantic scene.

ABOVE RIGHT: Large pipe organs like this one were installed in many early 20th-century cinemas.

THE SOUND ERA

When sound for movies was invented in the late 1920s, cinemagoers heard characters speak and sing for the first time. Composers created theme tunes to get audiences excited at the start of a movie as well as 'incidental music' which played during scenes. Incidental music tries to convey something about a character or the action. In horror movies and thrillers, music is often used to build up a feeling of suspense.

A pianist accompanies the film.

John Williams
Jaws theme tune

Elmer Bernstein
The Magnificent Seven theme tune

Danny Elfman
The Simpsons theme tune

ABOVE: *The Simpsons* TV show has a very catchy theme.

TV THEME TUNES

Many TV shows have theme tunes. Like film themes, they try to give some idea of what the show is about. For instance, light-hearted music is often used for comedies or game shows, whereas serious music features in dramas or documentaries. This music is often designed to be catchy and instantly recognizable, so that people remember the show and tune in again.

{ WRITING FILM MUSIC }

The most important part of writing music for films is timing, making sure that the sounds fit the visuals exactly. To do this, the composer uses a computer programme that times each scene and piece of action, so that they can compose their score to match. The music is then carefully recorded to make sure it is precisely the right length.

CASE STUDY: JOHN WILLIAMS

The composer John Williams (b. 1932) has written some of the most famous and recognizable film music of all time, including the scores to *Jaws*, *Star Wars*, *ET*, *Jurassic Park* and three of the *Harry Potter* films. He often composes themes known as leitmotifs, which play whenever a particular character appears. These include the eerie 'dah–da, dah–da' cello part for the shark in the film *Jaws*, and the sinister 'Imperial March' for Darth Vader in the *Star Wars* films.

RIGHT: The film *Jaws* was released in 1975.

BELOW: Darth Vader is a character in the *Star Wars* films.

WRITTEN MUSIC

IN ANCIENT TIMES, MUSICIANS LEARNT SONGS BY COPYING OTHER MUSICIANS. But by the Middle Ages people had come up with ways of writing music down, using symbols that corresponded to the pitch and rhythm of the notes. This allowed musicians to play songs they'd never heard before. Musical notation, as it's known, became more and more complex as time went on, so that every part of a performance could be written down.

ABOVE: Men perform on traditional drums in Ghana.

ORAL TRADITION

Before written and recorded music, songs were passed around orally. One musician would teach another musician a piece of music, note by note; they would then teach someone else, and so on. But some musicians would play a song differently or even add their own parts. In this way, songs evolved over time. The oral tradition still forms an important part of the musical cultures of Africa and Asia.

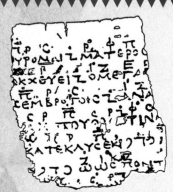

FAR LEFT: Fragment of musical notation from ancient Greece.

LEFT: A hymn written in Byzantine musical notation.

RIGHT: French mass book showing 13th-century musical notation.

THE FIRST WRITTEN MUSIC

Markings on a 3,000-year-old clay tablet from Mesopotamia are the earliest known written music. In around the 5th century BCE, the ancient Greeks developed a more accurate way of writing music. It took the form of symbols written above the words of a song, showing the pitch of each note. Using preserved manuscripts, it's possible for modern singers to recreate the songs of ancient Greece.

MEDIEVAL WRITTEN MUSIC

In the Middle Ages, musicians from the Byzantine Empire (in Eastern Europe and the Middle East) and Western Europe developed simple forms of musical notation. The symbols didn't show the exact pitch or length of notes, just the points where they got higher or lower. In European monasteries, monks used these symbols to help them remember religious songs known as plainchant.

MUSICAL NOTATION

In the 11th century, the system that would become modern musical notation was invented by an Italian monk called Guido d'Arezzo. He used four horizontal lines with spaces in between to indicate pitch. The position of a symbol on or between these lines showed the musician what note to play. Over the next few centuries, symbols were developed to show the length of each note.

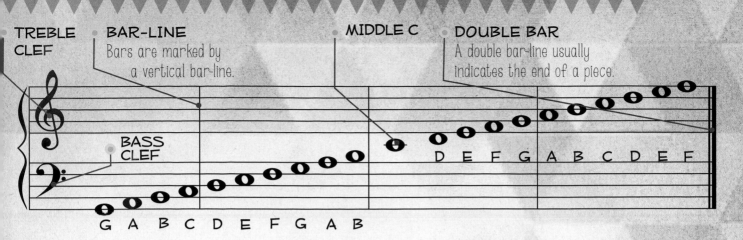

TREBLE CLEF

BAR-LINE Bars are marked by a vertical bar-line.

MIDDLE C

DOUBLE BAR A double bar-line usually indicates the end of a piece.

BASS CLEF

D E F G A B C D E F

G A B C D E F G A B

STAVES AND CLEFS

In modern Western music, notes are written on a set of five lines known as a **stave**. A sign called a **clef**, written at the start of a piece of music, tells the musician which lines stand for which notes. There are two main clefs: the treble clef for high notes and the bass clef for low ones.

NOTES AND BEATS

The shape of the note symbol tells the musician how long to hold the note. Notes are held according to a series of steady counts called beats. A crotchet is held for one beat, a minim for two beats and so on. The length of a beat isn't an exact time – like the length of a second – and can change slightly from musician to musician.

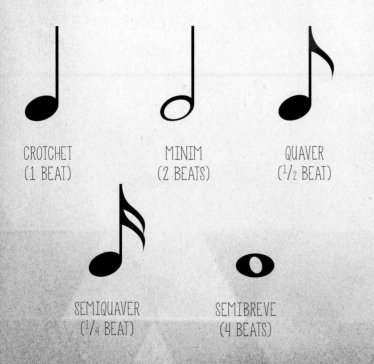

CROTCHET (1 BEAT)

MINIM (2 BEATS)

QUAVER (½ BEAT)

SEMIQUAVER (¼ BEAT)

SEMIBREVE (4 BEATS)

TIME SIGNATURES

Most music is made up of repeated patterns of beats. Each pattern is divided into a section called a bar. The type of pattern is indicated at the start of the piece by a time signature. This consists of two numbers, one written above the other. The lower figure shows what type of beat is being used (4 means a crotchet beat, 8 means a quaver beat and so on). The top figure tells you how many beats there are per bar.

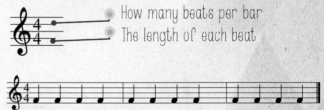

How many beats per bar
The length of each beat

ABOVE: 4/4 – Here there are four crotchet beats per bar. 4/4 is the most common time signature, which is why it's also known as 'common time'.

ABOVE: 3/4 – This indicates there are three crotchet beats per bar. This signature is often used in waltzes when it's counted *one*-two-three, *one*-two-three, *one*-two-three.

ABOVE: 2/2 – This signature indicates there are two minim beats per bar.

ABOVE: 6/8 – This indicates there are six quaver beats per bar. 6/8 is often used in jigs.

THE FIRST RECORDS

FOR MOST OF HUMAN HISTORY, MUSIC WAS ONLY HEARD LIVE.

Beginning with Thomas Edison's invention of the phonograph in the 1870s, it became possible to record and reproduce sounds. For the first time, people could listen to music in their own home and choose what they listened to. These early recordings weren't of a very high quality, with scratchy, muffled sound. But as the decades passed, recording technology got better, as did the equipment for replaying the sound.

ABOVE: A barrel organ in the early 1900s.

MECHANICAL INSTRUMENTS

The first music that was not a live performance was not a recording, but was produced by a machine. In the 9th century, the Banū Mūsā brothers from Baghdad were the leading inventors of the day. Their inventions included a steam-powered flute and a mechanical organ. Further mechanical instruments, including barrel organs, musical boxes and church bells, were later created in medieval Europe.

ABOVE: Player piano rolls in their boxes.

PLAYER PIANO

In the late 19th century, a piano that played itself was invented. It looked like a normal upright piano, but inside, mechanical equipment played notes according to holes punched in a roll of paper. Player pianos remained popular up until the 1920s, when the quality of sound recordings began to improve.

ABOVE: A 1902 player piano operated by pedals.

RIGHT: Thomas Edison and his phonograph in around 1877.

THE PHONOGRAPH

The phonograph was created by the celebrated US inventor Thomas Edison in 1877. It was the first device to both record and reproduce sound. It consisted of a cylinder covered in tin foil (later wax) on which a **stylus** etched grooves to record sounds. When a stylus was traced back over the groove, the vibrations could be amplified to reproduce the sounds.

GRAMOPHONE

Phonograph machines and cylinder recordings of music proved very popular. However, from 1889 onwards the technology had a rival: the gramophone. Invented by the German-American inventor Emile Berliner, it used discs rather than cylinders. Discs were easier to make, transport and store, and with two sides they had a greater playing time. They soon outsold cylinders.

ABOVE: Performers sing into a microphone at a recording session in 1916.

ABOVE: Early gramophones had a horn to amplify the sound.

ACOUSTIC RECORDING

The early recording process was simple. Musicians played together into a large horn. The sound waves vibrated the stylus, which cut directly into the wax on the cylinder (or disc). This created a **master recording**, from which copies could be made. The sound quality wasn't very good. Very low or very high notes often weren't recorded, or only faintly. This was known as acoustic recording.

RIGHT: A BBC microphone from around 1933.

DID YOU KNOW?

78s were made of shellac, a resin derived from South East Asian insects. It made the discs hard but brittle.

BELOW: An early 78 rpm record.

ELECTRICAL RECORDING

In the 1920s, electrical recording took over from acoustic recording. Electrical recording increased both the range of notes that could be recorded and the quality of the recordings. It followed the invention of the microphone, which converts sound into an electrical signal. This signal can be amplified, resulting in fuller-sounding, louder recordings. Electric gramophones soon followed, with the horn replaced by an amplifier and loudspeaker.

THE 78

To be played, a gramophone record had to be spun on a turntable beneath a stylus at a constant speed of 78 rpm (revolutions per minute). From the 1910s to the early 1950s, the 78 rpm disc was the standard format for nearly all records. It came in two main sizes: 12 in (30 cm), which lasted about 5 minutes per side, and 10 in (25 cm), which lasted about 3 minutes.

FROM VINYL TO THE WALKMAN

THE LATE 1940s AND 1950s SAW A NUMBER OF TECHNOLOGICAL INNOVATIONS.
The introduction of microgroove vinyl discs led to the development of singles and long-playing albums. Magnetic tape and **multitrack** recording enabled musicians to correct their mistakes and to build up a piece of music in layers rather than recording everything live. Many records were no longer representations of a live piece of music, but creations made solely in the studio.

Listen To Me Buddy Holly

ABOVE: The sound quality of an LP was much better than that of a 78.

THE LONG PLAYER

In 1948, a new type of record was introduced – a 12 in (30 cm) disc made of a durable, flexible plastic called vinyl. Its grooves were much finer than those of a 78, and it could be played slower, at 33.3 rpm. This meant that each side had 30 minutes of playing time, which is why it was called the long player (or LP).

RIGHT: A 1954 red vinyl record of Elvis Presley's *You're a Heartbreaker.*

SUN
Hi-Lo Music
BMI
Vocal
U-141
YOU'RE A HEARTBREAKER
(Jack Sallee)
ELVIS PRESLEY
SCOTTY and BILL
215
MEMPHIS, TENNESSEE

ABOVE: The musician Pete Townshend using magnetic tape.

SINGLES

1949 saw another format innovation – the 7-inch (18 cm) record, which was played at 45 rpm and could hold around five minutes of music per side. From the early 1950s onwards, it became the main way of selling individual songs of popular music, known as singles. Sales figures for singles were published as the pop charts. Vinyl LPs and singles would be the most popular formats for recorded music right up until the 1980s.

MAGNETIC TAPE

Recordings improved dramatically with the introduction of magnetic tape in the 1940s. Sound waves could be recorded on to acetate (a type of plastic) in a magnetic pattern. This had huge advantages over previous recording methods. Songs could be recorded, erased and recorded again on the same tape without reducing quality. Mistakes could be covered up by splicing together different sections of tape.

MULTITRACKING

In the early 1950s, the American musician Les Paul invented multitrack recording. This allowed different tracks (parts) of a song to be recorded separately on to the same section of tape. It was possible to record and edit each track separately. The tracks could then be played back together to create the whole song. Multitracking allowed musicians to create dense pieces of music made up of many different parts that couldn't possibly have been played at the same time.

DID YOU KNOW?

In the UK, recorded music only began to outsell sheet music in the 1950s. In the first UK pop chart in 1949, the positions were based on sheet music sales, not record sales.

RIGHT: A Sony Walkman cassette player with headphones.

ABOVE: Blank cassette tapes ready to be recorded on to.

HOME TAPING

Magnetic tape found its way into homes when compact tapes were introduced in the mid-1960s. Pre-recorded tapes were available along with blank cassettes. For the first time, people could record music for themselves – from the radio, from vinyl records or from other tapes. Compact tapes became a popular format and could also be used to listen to music outside the home.

THE WALKMAN

In 1979, Japan's Sony Corporation unveiled the Walkman, the first personal stereo system. This miniature machine allowed people to walk around listening to taped music through a pair of headphones. The company went on to sell nearly 400 million Walkmans around the world.

FROM
CDs TO MP3s

TECHNOLOGICAL INNOVATIONS IN THE 1980s CHANGED HOW MUSIC WAS RECORDED AND LISTENED TO.
The introduction of digital recording led to compact discs (CDs), which were harder-wearing and easier to use than vinyl records. But the CD's dominance was challenged in the 21st century by the arrival of **MP3s**, tiny digital files that could be downloaded from the internet. In just a few decades, the average person's record collection had shrunk from an entire wall of shelves to tiny digital files that could fit on a microchip.

ABOVE: A band recording a CD in a studio.

DIGITAL RECORDING

In the 1970s, a new method of recording was developed. The previous **analogue** system had involved producing a continuous pattern on to a magnetic tape that matched the sound waves of the music. **Digital recording** converted the sound waves into a long series of numbers. These could be recorded on to CDs, tapes and (later) computers.

LEFT: A compact disc is made of metal and covered in plastic.

RIGHT: A vintage hi-fi music system with a record player, a tape deck and a CD player.

COMPACT DISCS

By the late 1990s, vinyl records had been largely replaced by CDs – thin, circular sheets of metal covered in tiny indentations called 'pits'. A CD player uses a laser to scan the disc's surface, reading the pits. The size and arrangement of these pits is converted into a series of numbers. The player then turns these numbers into sound waves to play the music.

CDs V LPs

CDs have several advantages over vinyl records. Records can easily be scratched and dust on the surface can make the stylus jump. CDs have a plastic covering, which makes them much sturdier and less affected by dust. They are also much easier to use than records. Changing tracks on a vinyl record involves carefully moving a stylus into position. Changing tracks on a CD means simply pressing a button.

ABOVE: Personal computers can store thousands of records.

COMPUTER MUSIC

Until around 2000, hardly any music was stored on computers. Digital music files were very large and computers had much less memory than they do now. But then a new type of digital data file emerged, the MP3. It reduced a music file size by almost 10 times by removing those parts of the audio frequency that people normally can't hear. While the average song on a CD takes up 40MB, an MP3 song file takes up just 4MB.

MP3 PLAYERS

The invention of MP3s led to the development of a new type of personal stereo, the MP3 player. The earliest MP3 players, introduced in the late 1990s, had just 32MB of memory, enough for about eight songs. They were also bulky and expensive. But improvements in technology and increases in computer memory meant that, within a few years, MP3 players eventually had 40GB of memory – enough for 10,000 songs.

LEFT: A portable MP3 player with headphones.

BELOW: A UK record shop selling both vinyl records and CDs.

MUSIC DOWNLOADS

The combination of MP3 files, the increase in the average computer's memory and – most importantly – the spread of the internet has completely changed the way music is bought. Until the end of the 20th century, most music was bought in record shops. In the 21st century, online music stores have enabled consumers to download tracks directly as digital files. Music no longer has to take the form of a physical object.

THE RECORDING STUDIO

ADVANCES IN TECHNOLOGY MEAN THAT MUSIC CAN NOW BE RECORDED ALMOST ANYWHERE, INCLUDING IN YOUR OWN HOME USING A PERSONAL COMPUTER. Professional musicians, however, usually work in recording studios. These are filled with hi-tech equipment designed to get the best possible results. Recording can be a long process, as songs and pieces of music are slowly put together track by track and then mixed together to produce the end product.

ABOVE: A sound engineer at work.

THE LIVE ROOM

Most professional recording studios are divided into separate rooms. Each is carefully soundproofed to make sure that noise doesn't bleed from one to another when recording is in progress. The 'live room' is where the instruments and amplifiers are set up, and where the musicians perform during a recording session.

BELOW: A vocalist, two guitarists and a drummer rehearse in a recording studio.

THE CONTROL ROOM

Another important room is the 'control room' where recordings are made by technicians known as sound engineers. This room has lots of equipment for recording and manipulating sound, and powerful computers for storing the recordings. Engineers speak to the musicians in the live room via an intercom.

ISOLATION BOOTH

The studio may also contain an 'isolation booth' where particularly loud or prominent instruments, such as drums, electric guitars and vocals, can be recorded in a soundproof environment. These instruments are recorded on their own, so that their sound doesn't drown out the rest of the music.

BELOW: A drummer plays in the isolation booth.

RECORDING

Music used to be recorded live with all the musicians playing together. Modern music is usually recorded track by track. Each track is made up of just one part of a song – such as the drums, the bass line or the vocals. These tracks can then be combined for the final piece of music. When a musician adds to a song, a recording of the existing parts will be played to them through headphones so they can keep time.

MIXING

Once all the tracks have been recorded, they are then mixed together to create the final song, or master, from which copies can be made. To make sure the levels, tone and sound quality are right, the sound engineer may use a mixing desk (or mixing console). This can be used to control the volume, bass and **treble** of every track, carefully blending them together to form the final song.

ABOVE: An orchestra recording live in a studio.

BELOW: The console of a modern-day mixing desk.

RECORDING LIVE

Many orchestral performances are still recorded 'live' with all the musicians playing at the same time. To make sure the recording sounds as much like the live orchestra as possible, microphones need to be carefully positioned. It's important to get a balance, so that every section of the orchestra records at an equal volume.

ANCIENT MUSIC

THE EARLIEST MUSIC PROBABLY CONSISTED OF PEOPLE SINGING TO EACH OTHER WHILE STRIKING LOGS AND STICKS, OR CLAPPING TO KEEP A BEAT. But it wasn't long before humans began creating simple instruments, such as flutes and trumpets, from animal horns and bone. All early civilizations – including the Egyptians, the Chinese and the Greeks – invented music independently, showing how important it has been to the development of humankind.

SUGGESTED LISTENING

Michael Levy
An Ancient Lyre –
Echoes of the Ancient World

Atrium Musicae de Madrid
Musique de la Grèce Antique

ANCIENT FLUTES

Forty-thousand-year-old flutes made of birds' bones and mammoth tusks have been discovered in southern Germany. Historians believe that music and art played a major role in the culture of early *Homo sapiens*. Explorers found that the walls of caves were covered with prehistoric paintings.

RIGHT: Native American flute carved from animal bone.

ANCIENT STRINGS

Stringed instruments have been around for nearly as long as wind instruments. The earliest known examples are some 2,500-year-old lyres found in a royal tomb in Mesopotamia. They have wooden frames and animal-gut strings, and are adorned with precious stones and gold, showing that they belonged to wealthy people. Stringed instruments were also used by the ancient Egyptians and Greeks.

RIGHT: Replica of the Lyre of Ur, the oldest known stringed instrument.

ANCIENT EGYPTIAN MUSIC

Around 3000BCE, Egyptians were making tuned instruments, such as pipes made of reeds. By around 1500BCE musicians could choose from many more instruments, including lyres, drums carved from hollow logs, and trumpets and flutes made of bronze. Music was used to worship gods and as a form of entertainment. Groups of musicians would often play for the pharaoh (ruler).

BELOW: A wall painting showing ancient Egyptian stringed instruments.

ANCIENT GREEK MUSIC

The ancient Greeks were passionate about music. It was also an important part of plays performed on open-air stages. During a play, a group of performers called the 'chorus' would sing about the action taking place on stage. By around 300BCE, the Greeks had invented a way to write down music. They used mathematical formulas to work out the intervals between notes.

LEFT: A Greek chorus sings out from behind striking masks.

ANCIENT ROMAN MUSIC

Music was played at almost all Roman social occasions: at religious festivals, funerals and to accompany gladiators fighting in the arena. Roman instruments included the three-stringed lute; the cornu, a large, curved trumpet that wrapped around the body; and the hydraulis, or water organ, which used water to push air through tuned pipes, producing sounds.

LEFT: Roman musicians playing a hydraulis and a cornu.

ANCIENT CHINESE MUSIC

According to Chinese legends, music was invented in around 2500BCE by a man called Ling Lun, who made bamboo pipes to reproduce the sound of birdsong. From this he devised the pentatonic (five-note) scale used in much Chinese music. By around 1000BCE, music was very popular in China. The main instruments were flutes, tuned metal bells and a seven-stringed instrument called a guqin.

LEFT: Playing the guqin at a Chinese temple ceremony.

DID YOU KNOW?

The word 'music' comes from the Greek word *mousike*, which means 'art of the muses'. The muses were the ancient Greek goddesses of music, art and dance.

MEDIEVAL AND RENAISSANCE MUSIC (500–1600)

MUSIC CHANGED GREATLY IN EUROPE DURING THE MIDDLE AGES AND THE RENAISSANCE.

In the early Middle Ages, music was fairly simple, and consisted mainly of vocal music composed for the Church. As time went on, non-religious music also became popular. Musical styles grew more complex, particularly during the Renaissance. New instruments were invented, leading to more instrumental pieces being written.

ABOVE: A 13th-century manuscript shows a troubadour entertaining two princesses.

PLAINCHANT TO POLYPHONY

The earliest church music, known as plainchant, was performed by monks who sang a basic melody without musical accompaniment. Over time, the music became more intricate, and additional parts were added. By around 1150, it had evolved into polyphony, a type of music where two or more melodies are sung (or played) at the same time.

ABOVE: The *Montpellier Codex*, a collection of 13th- and 14th-century music manuscripts.

ABOVE: A medieval stringed instrument called a dulcimer.

MINSTRELS

Minstrels, also known as jongleurs, were medieval popular musicians. They travelled around, performing in villages and in the homes and castles of royals and nobles. Their songs were often about legends and historic events. In the 12th and 13th centuries, French minstrels called troubadours sang songs about chivalry and love, which were popular themes in the Middle Ages.

MEDIEVAL AND RENAISSANCE INSTRUMENTS

Most music in the Middle Ages was composed for singers using instruments similar to ancient ones. They included wooden flutes and recorders; plucked instruments, such as small harps, lutes and dulcimers; and early versions of the violin, the trombone (sackbut), and the oboe (shawm). As new instruments emerged in the Renaissance, including the violin, guitar and harpsichord, more instrumental music was composed.

DID YOU KNOW?

The English king Henry VIII was an enthusiastic musician and composer. He wrote dozens of pieces and had a large collection of musical instruments.

THE RENAISSANCE

From around 1300, people in Europe (especially in Italy) became much more interested in art and science, inspired by the cultures of ancient Greece and Rome. This period became known as the Renaissance, meaning 'rebirth'. Music grew more sophisticated, using more chords and harmony – a style known as homophony. Musicians began to write long pieces of music, unaccompanied by voices, which were the forerunners of the symphonies and concertos (see page 43) of later centuries.

LEFT: A 16th-century painting shows Italian Renaissance musicians.

PRINTING

Before the invention of the printing press in around 1450, pieces of music had to be written out by hand. This took a long time and usually meant that just a few copies were made. Printing was much faster and could produce many copies, allowing popular pieces of music to spread far and wide. This led to a demand for more music.

LEFT: Printing presses in the late 1500s.

THE REFORMATION

In the 16th century, during a period known as the Reformation, religious music changed. Until this time, church music had been sung by the clergy in Latin, the official language of the Church. However, some people believed the Catholic Church had become corrupt and founded a new type of Christianity called Protestantism. In Protestant churches, music was sung by everyone, religious leaders and congregation alike, often in their own language.

ABOVE: A 16th-century woodcut shows men and boys singing in church.

SUGGESTED LISTENING

Benedictine Monks of the Abbey of Santo Domingo de Silos
Sacred Chant: A Beautiful Collection of Gregorian Chants

Harry Christophers and The Sixteen
Christmas Music from Medieval and Renaissance Europe

41

BAROQUE
MUSIC (1600–1750)

BELOW: A bass line showing the notation for figured-bass harmony.

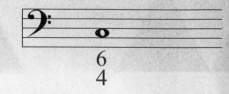

6
4

IN THE BAROQUE PERIOD, ART AND ARCHITECTURE BECAME VERY ORNATE AND ELABORATE.

The same thing happened in music, as composers began using complicated melodies, fast, complex rhythms, and contrasting sounds. In simple terms, music became much more 'twiddly'. Composers became increasingly ambitious and wrote longer pieces for larger groups of instruments. The orchestra as we know it today emerged, as did some of the most popular orchestral styles, including the concerto, the sonata and the suite.

HARMONY

Medieval music was mainly based on melodies made up of individual notes. The Baroque period marked a shift towards combinations of notes using chords and harmonies. Early harmonies often involved the use of basso continuo or 'figured bass'. This was a way of writing music using notes for the bass part but adding symbols and numbers below the stave to show what notes should be used to form chords.

ABOVE: An illustration of an ornate, Baroque, 18th-century concert hall in Venice.

ABOVE: A performance of Handel's *Messiah*.

PUBLIC CONCERTS

Following the Reformation, the Church's political control over Europe weakened, and there was a huge growth in non-religious music. Composers began writing instrumental music designed to be heard for its own sake. Public concerts, attracting paying members of the public, began to become common. Composers tried to use music to convey moods and feelings and so affect the emotions of listeners.

RELIGIOUS MUSIC

Baroque composers carried on writing religious music and used their new knowledge of harmony to create big, bold pieces, such as Bach's *St Matthew's Passion* and Handel's *Messiah*. These were played by large orchestras and choirs, and were designed to fill audiences with awe and wonder.

Handel
Messiah and *Zadok the Priest*

J. S. Bach
Toccata and Fugue in D minor;
and *Air on the G string
from Orchestral Suite no. 3*

Pachelbel
Canon in D

ABOVE: A modern Baroque orchestra with a harpsichord and lute.

THE ORCHESTRA

Before the Baroque era, music was usually vocal or played with whatever instruments were at hand. Now came a new idea: that certain pieces of music should be played by certain instruments, grouped in particular ways. This gave rise to the first orchestras. Baroque orchestras featured harpsichords (the main keyboard instrument of the period) violins, cellos, bassoons, oboes, trumpets and drums.

THE NEW MUSIC

Several new musical forms emerged in the Baroque period which are still played today. These include:

- **Concerto** – *A piece of music where a solo instrument (such as a flute) is accompanied by an orchestra. It often features a tricky part called a cadenza where a soloist shows off their skill.*

- **Sonata** – *A composition for a single instrument, usually a keyboard, or another instrument accompanied by a keyboard.*

- **Cantata** – *A piece of music written to be sung, usually by a choir, with a musical accompaniment and often made up of several movements.*

- **Oratorio** – *A bit like an opera but usually not staged, an oratorio is made up of instrumental and vocal music performed by an orchestra, choir and soloists.*

- **Suite** – *A compilation of instrumental pieces, usually high-tempo numbers, designed to be played one after the other.*

DID YOU KNOW?

The term 'Baroque' comes from the Portuguese word for a misshapen pearl.

J. S. BACH

MASTER OF THE BAROQUE

Johann Sebastian Bach was born in Germany in 1685 to a musical family. As a child, he could play both the violin and the harpsichord. Bach grew up to become a successful composer. He wrote an enormous amount of music, but his style had fallen out of fashion by the time he died in 1750. Today he is one of the most celebrated of all Baroque composers.

THE CLASSICAL PERIOD (1750–1820)

THE TERM 'CLASSICAL MUSIC' HAS TWO MEANINGS. It can be used to describe any music played by orchestras and small **ensembles**, using traditional instruments. But it can also refer to a particular period in Western orchestral music that came after the Baroque period. Classical music was in some ways simpler than Baroque music. But it was also bigger, played by larger orchestras, and more clearly based on tunes. This era also saw the number of public performances increase as ordinary people grew more interested in music.

THE CLASSICAL AGE

As with the Renaissance and Baroque periods, the Classical age influenced more than music. It saw the emergence of a new artistic movement based on the 'classical' styles of Greece and Rome. It also coincided with a period of great scientific advances known as the Enlightenment, and a number of revolutions (notably in France and the Americas) when the power of kings was being challenged by ordinary people. All these influences were reflected in Classical music.

ABOVE: The handwritten score of Mozart's Symphony no. 38 (Prague).

LEFT: The Austrian composer Wolfgang Amadeus Mozart around 1780 at the age of 24.

MELODY

There was a greater emphasis on melody in the Classical period than in previous times. Audiences began to favour music they could hum along to. Composers such as Mozart (see page 53) and Haydn who could write catchy tunes became very successful. They composed epic orchestral pieces with big, powerful sounds but also distinct melodies played over chords.

SUGGESTED LISTENING

Mozart
Eine Kleine Nachtmusik;
Symphony no. 40 in G major;
Queen of the Night Aria
from The Magic Flute

Haydn
Symphony no. 94 (Surprise);
Trumpet Concerto in E flat

BIG MUSIC

Music sounded bigger in the Classical period than it had ever done before, as the small, mainly string-based ensembles of the Baroque period gave way to much larger orchestras. The Classical period saw woodwind and brass sections added. The make-up of the orchestra has remained more or less the same to this day.

THE PIANO

In the Classical era, the piano took over from the harpsichord as the main keyboard instrument. Harpsichords could play bright, lively music but the piano, which was invented around 1700, was more versatile. It could play a loud melody, but could also be used for softer, gentler passages.

RIGHT: The colour of the keys on 18th-century pianos were sometimes the reverse of today's pianos.

RIGHT: A portrait of the composer Joseph Haydn (1732–1809).

BELOW: Sheet music of Haydn's *Spring* from *The Seasons*.

SMALL MUSIC

Growing interest in all forms of music meant that along with large orchestras, small groups also became popular. Many performed in small rooms (or chambers), which is why the music came to be called chamber music. One of the most well-liked small groups was the string quartet, which consisted of two violins, a viola and a cello.

BELOW: A classic string quartet.

NEW MUSIC

The symphony was the most significant musical development of the era. A symphony is divided into three or four movements. It usually features contrasting passages of quick, slow, loud and quiet music designed to utilize the whole orchestra. The **overture**, a one-movement piece played by a full orchestra, also emerged at this time. Overtures were originally written to introduce operas, but soon became popular in their own right.

THE ROMANTIC PERIOD (1820–1910)

THE CLASSICAL ERA WAS FOLLOWED BY THE ROMANTIC.
This period was in part a reaction to the Industrial Revolution, which had seen the growth of factories and cities across Europe. Romantic music took its inspiration from nature and ancient myths and legends. Composers tried to express powerful emotions, such as love, hate and grief (and later patriotism) through passionate and dramatic music. Pieces were often written to include **virtuoso** performances by the era's most skilled musicians.

THE AGE OF ROMANTICISM

During the Romantic period in Europe, composers began creating works based on ancient legends. In particular, the German composer Richard Wagner (1813–83), turned mythological subjects into grand emotional operas that reinvented the art form. Previously, there had been clear gaps between the musical pieces in an opera, but Wagner's operas just kept on going. His most famous composition, a set of four operas based on German mythology called *Der Ring des Nibelungen*, takes 18 hours to perform.

THE AGE OF INVENTION

Although Romantic music was often inspired by nature and ancient legends, it was also fiercely modern. Composers began to experiment by adding unexpected twists, such as sudden key or rhythm changes, to their pieces to increase the drama, as in the *Unfinished Symphony* by Franz Schubert (1797–1828). The tone poem, a one-movement piece designed to tell a story through music, also emerged in this period.

ABOVE: An illustration of Brünnhilde, a character from Wagner's *Der Ring des Nibelungen*.

LEFT: The Austrian composer Franz Schubert.

ABOVE: A large orchestra plays a piece of Romantic music.

THE ROMANTIC ORCHESTRA

The orchestra, already pretty large in the Classical period, grew in the Romantic period. Composers added everything they could think of to their music to try and create more drama. Very low-sounding instruments, like contrabassoons and bass clarinets, and very high ones, like piccolos, were used to provide texture. Percussion sections used the bangs, crashes and ringing of drums, bells and triangles to give more excitement to pieces.

AGE OF THE VIRTUOSO

As well as experimenting with the rules of music, composers also began to write more complicated pieces to be played by the very best musicians of the age, known as virtuosos. Virtuosos often became major stars in their own right. People flocked to the performances of the Italian Niccolò Paganini (1782–1840), who was widely regarded as one of the most brilliant violinists of the age.

LEFT: The virtuoso violinist Niccolò Paganini.

RIGHT: A map showing the small kingdoms (in different colours) that made up Europe in 1801.

SUGGESTED LISTENING

Dvořák
New World Symphony

Tchaikovsky
Dance of the Sugar Plum Fairy
from The Nutcracker

Beethoven
Symphony no. 9
(the Choral)

NATIONALIST MUSIC

Prior to the 19th century, much of Europe was split into small kingdoms or formed part of larger empires. In the 1800s, many of the countries that we now know, such as Germany and Italy, emerged. Much of the music of this time was designed to stir feelings of national pride. Some composers, such as Russia's Pyotr Ilyich Tchaikovsky (1840–93), Finland's Jean Sibelius (1865–1957) and Poland's Frédéric Chopin (1810–49) wrote pieces based on the history and folk songs of their own countries.

THE 20TH CENTURY

SUGGESTED LISTENING

IN THE 20TH CENTURY, COMPOSERS BEGAN CHALLENGING THE OLD RULES OF MUSICAL COMPOSITION. They explored strange musical structures, creating pieces that sounded like nothing that had gone before. Some composers rejected the grand orchestral pieces of the 19th century to create minimalistic music using just a few notes. Others experimented with different instruments and even tried to come up with new ways of writing music. For audiences, the music was often strange and confusing to listen to – but it was certainly very new.

Claude Debussy
La Mer

Aaron Copland
Fanfare for the Common Man

John Cage
Music of Changes

IMPRESSIONISTS

The symphonies of the great Romantic composers, such as Beethoven, had clear, forceful melodies. But in the late 19th and early 20th century, some composers, such as Claude Debussy (1862–1918), began to create looser, more 'impressionistic' music. Just as Impressionist painters created images that weren't exact photo-like replicas of scenes but vague impressions, so composers tried to convey general moods and feelings rather than write traditional tunes.

THE RUSSIANS

Several Russian composers from the Soviet Union came to international attention in this period. They included Sergei Prokofiev (1891–1953), Dmitri Shostakovich (1906–75) and Igor Stravinsky (see page 55), who all composed pieces that mixed traditional with new music. They challenged their audiences with new sounds – sometimes a little too much; the premiere of Stravinsky's 1913 ballet *The Rite of Spring* ended in a near riot.

THE AMERICANS

In the US, George Gershwin (1898–1937) merged existing styles to create a new form – classical jazz – with his orchestral pieces *Rhapsody in Blue*, *An American in Paris* and the opera *Porgy and Bess*. Other noted US composers of this time included Aaron Copland (1900–90), Leonard Bernstein (1918–90) and Samuel Barber (1910–81).

LEFT: An Impressionist painting by Claude Monet of waterlilies from 1899.

LEFT: The score for Sergei Prokofiev's *Peter and the Wolf*, a piece designed to teach children about music.

ABOVE: Poster for the film *An American in Paris* scored by George Gershwin.

MINIMALIST MUSIC

Minimalist music was a reaction against the size, complexity and volume of 19th-century orchestral music. Composers such as Philip Glass (b. 1937) and Terry Riley (b. 1935) thought that big symphonies were too complicated for the audience to be able to concentrate on what was important. So they stripped everything away to produce hypnotic, haunting pieces based around a few notes and played on a handful of instruments.

ABOVE: Philip Glass rehearsing at an electric keyboard in 1977.

RIGHT: The Austrian composer Arnold Schoenberg.

SERIAL MUSIC

The Austrian Arnold Schoenberg (1874–1951) rejected almost everything about traditional music theory, and composed pieces using a mathematical formula. He helped develop **serial music**, in which composers use the 12 notes of a chromatic scale to create a pattern where each note is featured once. This pattern is then used to create an entire piece of music. The result can be discordant and, without a recognizable tune, difficult to follow.

STOCKHAUSEN

The German Karlheinz Stockhausen (1928–2007) was a very experimental composer. In his career, he worked on both aleatory and serial music and was a pioneer of electronic music, becoming one of the first composers to use synthesizers. He was constantly looking to incorporate new instruments and sounds into his music.

RIGHT: A cellist prepares to perform Stockhausen's *Helicopter String Quartet* in 2007.

EDITION PETERS
No. 6777

JOHN CAGE

4' 33"

ALEATORY MUSIC

Another experimental form, aleatory music, introduced chance into composition. It's not written like traditional music. Instead the composer notes down a few guidelines, but many of the music's features, such as the tempo, key and which notes to use, are decided by random elements, such as rolling dice. Indeed, the term 'aleatory' comes from the Latin '*Alea*', which means 'the rolling of dice'.

LEFT: The cover of John Cage's work *4' 33"*, which consists entirely of silence.

DID YOU KNOW?

Stockhausen's compositions were often very unusual. One of his final operas featured a camel and musicians playing in helicopters hovering above the audience.

BALLET AND OPERA

CLASSICAL MUSIC ISN'T ALWAYS ABOUT JUST WHAT YOU CAN HEAR. Throughout its history, it has been combined with other art forms, such as dance, in the form of ballet, and drama, in the form of opera. Ballet uses movements performed by dancers to tell a story accompanied by music. Opera is a drama in which the story is told using songs. Both often feature elaborate costumes and scenery. Some of the most acclaimed classical composers have written ballets and operas.

LEFT: King Louis XIV in his ballet costume as the 'Sun King' in 1653.

BALLET BEGINNINGS

Ballet began in aristocratic homes during the Italian Renaissance. Its popularity spread to France, where King Louis XIV (1638–1715) became a passionate supporter, performing in several ballets himself. Early ballets were accompanied by acting and singing, and were known as opera-ballets. In the 18th century, the opera element was dropped and ballet became its own art form. The story was told solely through dance, movement and mime.

ABOVE: *Swan Lake* performed in London by the Russian Bolshoi Ballet in 2006.

RUSSIAN BALLET

In the late 19th century, ballet's spiritual home moved from France to Russia. Here a more complicated style of ballet emerged, which was designed to showcase the dancers' supreme skills. Many of the most popular ballets of this period, including *Swan Lake* and *The Nutcracker*, had music written by the Russian composer Tchaikovsky.

ABOVE: Alexandra Timofeeva of the Kremlin Ballet performs to music by Stravinsky in *The Firebird*.

BALLETS RUSSES

From 1909 to 1929, the Paris-based Russian ballet company the Ballets Russes changed the way ballet was staged. Its shows placed as much emphasis on the music, story and stage design as on the technical abilities of the dancers. Some of the biggest names of the time, including Maurice Ravel (1875–1937), Igor Stravinsky (see page 55) and Claude Debussy, were hired to write music for the company. It had a huge influence on the development of modern ballet.

RIGHT: Venice's opera house La Fenice was rebuilt in 1837.

OPERA'S BEGINNINGS

Like ballet, opera began as a form of private entertainment for wealthy Italian nobles in the early 1600s. These musical plays featured simple, catchy songs and soon became hugely popular. By the mid-17th century, the first purpose-built opera houses had begun to pop up across Europe. Here, audiences came to socialize, chat and watch the latest performances.

OPERA SERIA AND OPERA BUFFA

In the 18th century, opera divided into two main forms. Opera seria was 'serious' opera in which highly moral stories were told based on ancient history and mythology. These operas often featured comic intermissions called intermezzi. Over time, the intermezzi became so popular that composers began creating entire comic operas known as 'opere buffe' in Italian.

ABOVE LEFT: Rossini's *The Barber of Seville*, an opera buffa.

LEFT: English National Opera performs Puccini's *Madame Butterfly*.

ROMANTIC OPERA

As with other forms of music, opera got bigger and more dramatic in the 19th century under the influence of Romanticism. Giuseppe Verdi (1813–1901), Giacomo Puccini (1858–1924) and, in particular, Richard Wagner (1813–83) composed long, epic pieces filled with emotion. But this era also saw the emergence of operetta – short, comic musical dramas with light-hearted stories and catchy, hummable melodies.

20TH-CENTURY OPERA

In the 20th century, composers began experimenting with traditional musical structures in opera. Composers such as Arnold Schoenberg (1874–1951) and Dmitri Shostakovich (1906–1975) used **atonality** and **dissonance** in their works. This provoked a backlash among some composers, including Stravinsky. They rejected **modernism** in favour of writing traditional music based on the styles and rules of the Classical era – this was known as **neoclassicism**.

SUGGESTED LISTENING

BALLET:
Tchaikovsky *The Nutcracker*
Stravinsky *The Firebird*

OPERA:
Rossini *Figaro's Aria* from *The Barber of Seville*
Puccini *Un bel di Vedremo* from *Madame Butterfly*

ANTONIO
VIVALDI

1678–1741

ALONG WITH BACH, VIVALDI IS ONE OF THE MOST CELEBRATED BAROQUE COMPOSERS.
Born in Venice, Vivaldi was taught to play the violin by his father while still a child. He showed such skill that father and son were soon putting on performances across the city. As an adult, he proved equally successful as a composer and was commissioned to write pieces by some of Europe's leading figures, including the French king Louis XV.

LEFT: Antonio Vivaldi holding a violin.

BELOW: A view of Venice painted by Canaletto in the 1730s.

VIVALDI'S BELIEFS

Religion was very important to Vivaldi and he originally trained to be a priest. Unfortunately, severe asthma prevented him from conducting religious services (or playing wind instruments). Instead, he spent his time playing the violin, and teaching and composing music.

VIVALDI'S WORLD

Vivaldi spent most of his life in Venice, which in the Middle Ages controlled a vast European trading empire. However, by the time Vivaldi arrived, the city's power was fading. Instead, it had begun to make a name for itself as a tourist centre. Aristocrats flocked to the city from all over Europe on 'grand tours' to see its historic architecture, attend a masked ball and, of course, hear the music of the great Vivaldi.

VIVALDI THE TEACHER

For several decades, Vivaldi was employed as a teacher at a girls' orphanage. Indeed, many of his most famous pieces were premiered by the school's musicians. Vivaldi wrote more than 500 concertos, dozens of operas and numerous pieces of church music. His best-known piece, *The Four Seasons*, composed in 1723, is a set of four violin concertos, each themed on a season.

LEFT: Score showing themes from *The Four Seasons*.

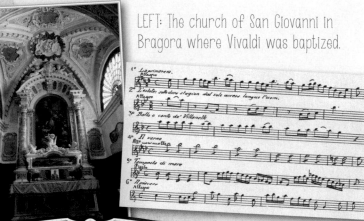

LEFT: The church of San Giovanni in Bragora where Vivaldi was baptized.

TIMELINE: VIVALDI

1678	1684–99	1703	1703	1713	1714–18	1723	1740	1741
Born in Venice	Venice goes to war with Ottoman Empire, emerging victorious	Ordained as a priest	Becomes a music teacher at the Ospedale della Pietà	First opera, *Ottone in Villa*, premiered	Venice loses Corfu and other territories in a war – city begins to decline	Composes *The Four Seasons*	Moves to Vienna, but is not as successful as he was in Venice	Dies in Vienna, probably of asthma

WOLFGANG AMADEUS MOZART

1756–1791

LEFT: The young Mozart at his harpsichord.

TODAY MANY PEOPLE CONSIDER MOZART TO BE THE GREATEST COMPOSER THAT EVER LIVED. A highly skilled instrumentalist by the age of four, he was taken by his father on tours around Europe where he wowed audiences with his incredible harpsichord and violin playing. As an adult, he composed a huge amount of music, much of it very popular. However, he was never able to make much money from his work and died, aged just 35, in poverty.

STANDING UP FOR THE POOR

Although he often wrote music for royalty, Mozart was critical of the upper classes. One of his most famous operas, *The Marriage of Figaro*, tells the story of a servant standing up to his boss. Mozart may have been influenced by the thinking of the time. He died shortly after the French Revolution, in which the poor people of France overthrew their rich, royal rulers.

THE MUSIC MASTER

Mozart was an incredibly talented musician. It was said that he could hear a piece of music just once and immediately play it from memory. He composed his first pieces when aged just five (which his father wrote down for him), had his first sonatas published at eight, and by eleven had completed his first opera. He continued writing at a tremendous rate for the rest of his life, eventually completing more than 600 pieces, including 41 symphonies.

ABOVE: A staging of Mozart's *The Marriage of Figaro*.

ABOVE: Mozart's piano.

TIMELINE: MOZART

1756	1763	1764	1767	1773	1781	1782	1786	1789	1791
Born in Salzburg, Austria	Tours Europe as a child musician	Writes first sonata, aged 8	First opera, *Apollo et Hyacinthus*, premiered, aged 11	Employed by the Archbishop of Salzburg	Moves to Vienna	Marries Constanze Weber	Premiere of *The Marriage of Figaro*	French Revolution sees France's poor overthrow their monarchy	Mozart's opera *The Magic Flute* opens. He dies three months later

LUDWIG VAN BEETHOVEN

1770–1827

BEETHOVEN WAS A SUPERSTAR OF HIS TIME AND TODAY IS ONE OF THE FEW COMPOSERS THAT ALMOST EVERYBODY HAS HEARD OF. Like Vivaldi and Mozart before him, Beethoven received his early musical instruction from his father. He lived most of his life in Vienna, Austria. There, supported by local noblemen, he gained a reputation as a virtuoso pianist and a gifted composer – as well as a difficult, argumentative character.

LEFT: Ludwig van Beethoven.

ABOVE: Beethoven's ear trumpet.

COMPOSING IN SILENCE

In his early 30s, Beethoven started to lose his hearing. The problem got steadily worse, and by 1814 he was totally deaf and had to use written notes to communicate with people. Nonetheless, he continued to compose up until his death. He also continued conducting his own work. Apparently, he thought the premiere of his *Ninth Symphony* had been a failure because he couldn't hear any applause. He had to be turned around so he could see the audience cheering.

THE NEW ROMANTIC

Beethoven is regarded as marking the transition from Classicism (pages 44–45) to Romanticism (pages 46–47). His works were long and required lots of musicians (his *Ninth Symphony* features both an orchestra and a full choir). Loud and very passionate, they were designed to provoke deep emotions in the audience. He wrote nine symphonies, five concertos for piano, 32 piano sonatas, 16 string quartets as well as many smaller works.

RIGHT: Emperor Napoleon.

THE HEROIC SYMPHONY

Despite being commissioned to write music by nobles, Beethoven supported the French Revolution and its anti-royalist ideals. He even named his third symphony in honour of Napoleon Bonaparte, who had become leader of France after the revolution. However, he changed its title to the *Eroica* ('Heroic') when Napoleon had himself crowned emperor in 1804.

RIGHT: Cover page of Beethoven's *Eroica*.

TIMELINE: BEETHOVEN

1770	1783	1789	1792	1800	1801	1804	1808	1827
Born in Bonn, Germany	First piece of music published, aged 13	French Revolution	Moves to Vienna, Austria, to study with Joseph Haydn	First symphony performed	Begins to go deaf	Napoleon Bonaparte becomes Emperor of France	Premieres what becomes his best-known symphony, the *Fifth*	Beethoven dies after a prolonged illness

IGOR STRAVINSKY

1882–1971

STRAVINSKY WAS A MUSICAL CHAMELEON, FOREVER CHANGING HIS STYLE.

During his long career, he tackled almost all of the 20th century's main forms of classical music, including modernist, neoclassical, ballet, opera and folk music. His most famous piece is *The Rite of Spring*, music for a ballet about Russian pagan rituals. It was considered so revolutionary that it almost caused a riot at its 1913 premiere in Paris.

ABOVE: Igor Stravinsky conducting in 1965.

EARLY CAREER

Born in St. Petersburg, Russia, Stravinsky grew up around music. His father was an opera singer and he began piano lessons aged nine. After training to be a lawyer, he tried his luck at composing. His first major success came following a move to Switzerland where he wrote scores for the Ballets Russes, a Paris-based Russian dance company. These pieces, which included *The Rite of Spring*, were acclaimed for their revolutionary use of unusual rhythms and dissonance.

ABOVE: The Béjart Ballet performing *The Rite of Spring*.

LEFT: Mikhail Baryshnikov and Susan Jaffe in *Apollo*, scored by Stravinsky.

CHANGING STYLES

In the 1920s, Stravinsky moved to France and changed his musical style. Here he wrote neoclassical music, which was based on the classical styles of previous centuries. Following the death of his wife from tuberculosis, he moved again in 1940 to the US where he lived for the rest of his life. In the 1950s, he changed styles again, writing serial music, which was pioneered by the avant-garde composer Arnold Schoenberg.

TIMELINE: STRAVINSKY

1882	1891	1901	1907	1910	1913	1920	1940	1953	1971
Born in St. Petersburg, Russia	Begins piano lessons	Begins studying law and receives diploma in 1906	First public performance of music	Moves to Switzerland	*The Rite of Spring* is premiered in Paris, provoking a near riot	Moves to Paris	Moves to the US	Begins writing serial music	Dies in New York, and is buried in Venice, Italy

BENJAMIN BRITTEN

1913–1976

BENJAMIN BRITTEN WAS ONE OF THE LEADING COMPOSERS OF THE 20TH CENTURY.

As well as composing numerous operas (both big and small), choral works, instrumental pieces and scores for films, he was also a highly skilled pianist and conductor.

ABOVE: Benjamin Britten with his dog Clytie.

RIGHT: Britten in his school uniform aged 10.

BELOW: *Grimes on the Beach* performed in 2013.

EARLY LIFE

Born in Suffolk on England's east coast, Britten became interested in music at a young age. In 1930, he won a scholarship to London's prestigious Royal College of Music, and afterwards spent much of his early career writing music for films and radio programmes. A committed pacifist (someone who refuses to fight in wars), Britten moved to the US in 1939, just before the outbreak of the Second World War.

PETER GRIMES

Feeling homesick, Britten returned to Suffolk in 1942, while the war was still going on. He was excused from military service by the Government, and spent the latter part of the conflict writing the opera that would make his name: *Peter Grimes*. It tells the tragic story of a Suffolk fisherman accused of killing his apprentice. First performed in June 1945, it was a huge hit and is still regularly staged today. *Grimes on the Beach* was performed outdoors on the very coast where Britten wrote the opera and set the story.

TIMELINE BRITTEN

1913	1914–18	1919	1921	1929	1930	1932	1939	1942
Born in Lowestoft, Suffolk	World War I	Writes first song	Starts piano lessons	Start of the Great Depression	Enters Royal College of Music	First work published	Moves to US; World War II begins	Returns to Britain

WORKS

In 1947, after the Second World War, Britten moved to the town of Aldeburgh with his partner, the singer Peter Pears. Over the next few decades, Britten wrote a number of acclaimed works, including the chamber opera *The Turn of the Screw*, the opera *Gloriana*, written to mark the coronation of Queen Elizabeth II, and the *War Requiem*, a piece that commemorates the dead of the century's two world wars.

LEFT: One of the 20th century's most popular operas, *The Turn of the Screw*, staged in 2013 by the New York City Opera.

BELOW: Britten and Pears at Snape Maltings in 1969.

ALDEBURGH FESTIVAL

In 1948, Britten helped to launch the annual Aldeburgh Festival. Originally intended as a showcase for opera, it grew over the years into a large-scale celebration of all types of classical music. Since 1967, the main venue has been Snape Maltings, a 19th-century brewery building that Britten turned into a concert hall.

FRIDAY AFTERNOONS

Throughout his career, Britten wrote pieces specifically for children with the aim of getting them interested in music. He composed *Friday Afternoons*, a collection of 12 songs based on short poems, for the school where his brother was headmaster. The pupils got together every Friday afternoon to sing them. A decade later, Britten composed *The Young Person's Guide to the Orchestra* (see pages 92–93) for an educational documentary to be shown in schools throughout the country.

RIGHT: 100,000 children worldwide sing Britten's *Friday Afternoons* as part of his centenary celebrations in 2013.

1945	1945 cont'd	1948	1953	1954	1962	1967	1973	1976
Peter Grimes premieres	World War II Ends	First Aldeburgh Festival	Coronation of Elizabeth II and the premiere of *Gloriana*	Premiere of the ghost-story opera *The Turn of the Screw*	Premiere of *War Requiem*	Snape Maltings Concert Hall opens	*Death in Venice*, Britten's final opera, opens	Dies at home of heart failure

THE ORCHESTRA

AN ORCHESTRA IS MADE UP OF A LARGE GROUP OF CLASSICAL MUSICIANS WHO ARE LED BY A CONDUCTOR. The instruments are divided into four sections: strings, wind, brass and percussion. Other instruments, such as piano and harp, also sometimes feature but are not usually regarded as part of these sections. The typical symphony orchestra has around 100 members, although there is no fixed figure. Some pieces require more musicians, some require fewer. Small orchestras of around 25 musicians are known as chamber orchestras.

DID YOU KNOW?

The world's biggest orchestra was gathered together in 2013 as part of the Queensland Music Festival in Australia. It was made up of 7,224 musicians and played Beethoven's *Ninth Symphony*.

HISTORY

The orchestra, as we now know it, emerged in the 17th century during the Baroque period (see pages 42–43) when composers first began writing music for specific instruments. Early orchestras were quite small, but grew significantly over the next few centuries as more instruments were added. By the early 19th century, with the average orchestra now made up of dozens of instruments, it became necessary to have a conductor to keep all the musicians playing together.

LEFT: The 18th-century Teatro Regio in Turin, Italy, with a small Baroque orchestra in front of the stage.

SET-UP

The orchestra is arranged in a semicircle around the conductor. The stringed instruments are at the front. Behind them are the wind instruments, then the brass instruments and, finally, at the back, the percussion instruments. Those instruments that aren't part of a standard orchestra – notably the piano and harp – are placed to the side of the main sections.

Harp & Piano

Brass

Percussion

Wind

Strings

Conductor

BALANCE

The orchestra is carefully arranged to get the best balance between the instruments. The violins are at the front and percussion is at the back because percussion instruments, such as the timpani, are much louder than the violins, and would overwhelm them if they were any closer. For the same reason, there are many more string instruments than there are wind or brass instruments.

HOW ORCHESTRAS WORK

The conductor (see pages 90–91) sets the tempo and directs the music. Musicians follow both the conductor's baton movements and the printed score on the music stand in front of them. The musicians don't always all play at the same time. There may be quiet passages where just a few instruments are used, as well as louder passages where many instruments combine. Musicians must pay careful attention to the score and the conductor to make sure they play at the right times.

LEFT: The conductor Leonard Slatkin uses his baton to lead an orchestra in 2010.

SOLOISTS AND LEADERS

Some orchestral pieces, such as concertos, feature a soloist as well as a full orchestra. The soloist plays complicated passages designed to showcase their skill. Every section of the orchestra has a principal, who plays the orchestral solos. The principal of the first violins is also known as the concertmaster or leader. They lead the tuning of the orchestra prior to a performance.

LEFT: A soloist plays the violin in a classical orchestra.

STRINGED INSTRUMENTS

THE SOUND OF A STRINGED INSTRUMENT IS PRODUCED BY THE VIBRATIONS OF ITS STRINGS. These vibrations are then either amplified by the body of the instrument (acoustically) or by an electrical signal. Stringed instruments are played in three main ways – by plucking or strumming the strings either with the fingers or with a pick (as with a guitar), by drawing a bow made of animal hair across the strings (as with a violin), or by striking the strings with an object (as with a piano).

ABOVE: Violins, cellos and double basses play together in the string section.

ORCHESTRAL STRINGS

There are between 40 and 60 stringed instruments in a modern symphony orchestra, making it by far the biggest section. The strings are further divided into four main groups: violins, violas, cellos and double basses. All are played using a combination of bow and fingers.

VIOLIN (see pages 62–63)
FROM: Italy
INVENTED: 16th century
STRINGS: 4

The orchestra's violins are divided into two sections: first violins, which play the main melodies; and second violins, which tackle the lower notes and rhythmic passages. There are more violins in an orchestra than any other instrument – typically ten first violins and ten second violins. Since the Classical period the principal violinist has been the leader of the orchestra.

VIOLA
FROM: Italy
INVENTED: 16th century
STRINGS: 4

The viola is a slightly bigger, slightly lower-sounding version of the violin, and is played in much the same way, held under the musician's chin. It occupies the middle range of the stringed instruments, tuned a fifth below the violin and an octave above the cello. There are around eight violas in a typical orchestra.

CELLO
FROM: Italy
INVENTED: 16th century
STRINGS: 4

The next biggest instrument in the orchestral string family, the cello is around 122 cm (48 in) long, making it far too big to be picked up and played under the chin. Instead it rests on the floor on an endpin that extends from the bottom of the instrument. The cellist (cello player) rests the instrument between their legs while they play. An orchestra usually has 10 cellos.

DOUBLE BASS

FROM: Italy

INVENTED: 16th century

STRINGS: 4

The double bass (also known as the string bass or contrabass) is the largest and lowest-sounding member of the string family. At 1.90 m (75 in), it's taller than most people and is rested on the floor during play. Depending on their height, the bass player can choose to either sit or stand when playing the instrument. An orchestra usually has six double basses.

THE HARP

(see pages 64–65)

FROM: France

INVENTED: 19th century

STRINGS: 47

The harp is an occasional addition to the symphony orchestra, and sits with the strings, positioned either behind or to the side of the violins. The harpist (harp player) sits next to it on a chair to play.

Acoustic Guitar
FROM: Spain
STRINGS: 6
INVENTED: 19th century

Electric Guitar
FROM: United States
STRINGS: 6
INVENTED: 1930s

Pedal Steel Guitar
FROM: Hawaii
STRINGS: 10–20
INVENTED: 19th century

Balalaika
FROM: Russia
STRINGS: 3
INVENTED: 17th century

Electric Bass
FROM: United States
STRINGS: 4–6
INVENTED: 1950s

Sitar
FROM: India
STRINGS: 18–20
INVENTED: 14th century

Banjo
FROM: United States
STRINGS: 5
INVENTED: 19th century

Mandolin
FROM: Italy
STRINGS: 8
(in 4 paired courses)
INVENTED: 18th century

Ukulele
FROM: Hawaii
STRINGS: 4
INVENTED: 19th century

Bouzouki
FROM: Asia Minor
STRINGS: 6–8 (in 3–4 paired courses)
INVENTED: c. 4th century BCE (brought to Greece in 1920s)

Oud (Lute)
FROM: Middle East
STRINGS: 11–13
INVENTED: c. 3000BCE

Zither
FROM: Central Europe
STRINGS: 29–42
INVENTED: 18th century

THE VIOLIN

MAKING A VIOLIN

A traditional violin is made of more than 70 separate pieces of wood. Each is carefully carved into the correct shape, stuck together with glue and covered in layers of varnish. The body is made first, and then it's attached to the neck. Finally, the bridge, tailpiece, tuning pegs and strings are added. Some modern violins are made of synthetic materials, such as plastic and fibreglass.

WITH ITS CURVY 'HOURGLASS' SHAPE, THE VIOLIN IS ONE OF THE WORLD'S MOST RECOGNIZABLE INSTRUMENTS. Also known as a 'fiddle', it is the smallest and highest-pitched member of the orchestra's string family. Using a bow, or plucking the strings with their fingers, a violinist can produce a great range of sounds. The violin is used in many different types of music, including country, folk and classical, and can be played as a solo instrument or as part of an orchestra.

BRIDGE
Transmits the strings' vibrations to the body, and is curved to allow the strings to be played individually.

FINGERBOARD

THE BOW

HAIR
A thin ribbon of real (or synthetic) horsehair is drawn over the strings to produce the violin's sound.

CHINREST

SUGGESTED LISTENING

Vivaldi
The Four Seasons

Tchaikovsky
Violin Concerto in D major

Stéphane Grappelli
'The Best of' album

TAILPIECE
Holds the strings in place and makes sure they are the right distance apart.

F-HOLES
Allow the sound vibrations inside the instrument to be transmitted to the air outside.

STRINGS
Tuned to four notes: G (the lowest), D, A and E (the highest).

RIGHT: Antonio Stradivari making violins in the 18th century.

THE STICK
Made from a strong, springy material, such as Brazilwood, the stick is slightly curved to hold the hair tight.

PEGS
Each string is wound around a wooden peg, which can be tightened to raise its pitch, or loosened to lower it.

NECK

BODY

INVENTING THE VIOLIN

The four-string violin was invented in Italy in the mid-16th century. It was based on earlier two- and three-stringed instruments. Over the next few centuries, it was developed into the instrument we know today. Apart from the materials used in its construction, the violin's design has changed little since the 18th century.

PLAYING THE VIOLIN

When the strings of a violin are plucked or played with a bow, they vibrate to make sound. This is made louder by the instrument's body. Different notes are made by pressing down the strings on the fingerboard. The closer the fingers are to the body of the instrument, the higher the note. The violin is held tightly between chin and shoulder, allowing the violinist's hands to move freely.

BELOW: A violinist plays in an orchestra.

DID YOU KNOW?

Violins are some of the world's most expensive instruments. The Lady Blunt Stradivarius made in 1721 by the Italian master instrument-maker Antonio Stradivari sold for $15.9 million at auction in 2011.

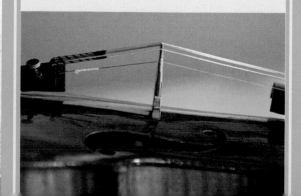

THE HARP

THE HARP IS *ONE OF THE OLDEST INSTRUMENTS.* Basic versions, consisting of strings stretched across a wooden frame, were recovered from a tomb in the Mesopotamian city of Ur, dating back to 2600BCE. The modern concert (or pedal) harp is just a few hundred years old and is a much larger and more complicated instrument. Harps can produce shimmering, waterfall-like effects of cascading notes as well as delicate, intricate melodies.

SUGGESTED LISTENING

Britten
Suite for Harp

Debussy
Suite for Flute, Violin and Harp

Mozart
Concerto for Flute and Harp

MAKING A HARP

Concert harps are usually made out of maple wood. The larger parts – the soundboard, soundbox, shoulder and neck – are put together first. The tuning pins, strings and pedals are then added. A full-size concert grand harp is very large, standing more than 1.8 m (6 ft) tall, and weighing around 40 kg (90 lb). It is so heavy it must rest on the floor, like a piano.

LEFT: A craftsman making a modern, hand-held harp.

STRINGS

The harp has 47 strings, giving it a range of six octaves. The lower strings are made of wound metal (steel or copper) while the higher strings are made of gut or nylon.

COLUMN

BASE

INVENTING THE HARP

Simple harps were invented around 5,000 years ago in the Middle East, before spreading to Europe. The large, floor harp was invented in the Renaissance, but it had a limited range. Pedals were added in the 17th century. They could be pressed with the feet to raise and lower the pitch of the strings. The Frenchman Sébastien Erard is generally credited with having invented the modern seven-pedalled harp in 1810.

LEFT: An ancient Egyptian wall painting shows an early harp.

TUNING PINS

To help harpists find their position, C strings are coloured red, and F strings are black.

SHOULDER

NECK

PLAYING THE HARP

Sounds are made by plucking the strings with the thumb and first three fingers of each hand. Little fingers are too weak to pluck and are never used. The note of each string can be changed by using one of seven pedals – three controlled with the left foot, four controlled with the right. These pedals change the length of the string, allowing the harpist to play the **flat**, **natural** and **sharp** versions of each note.

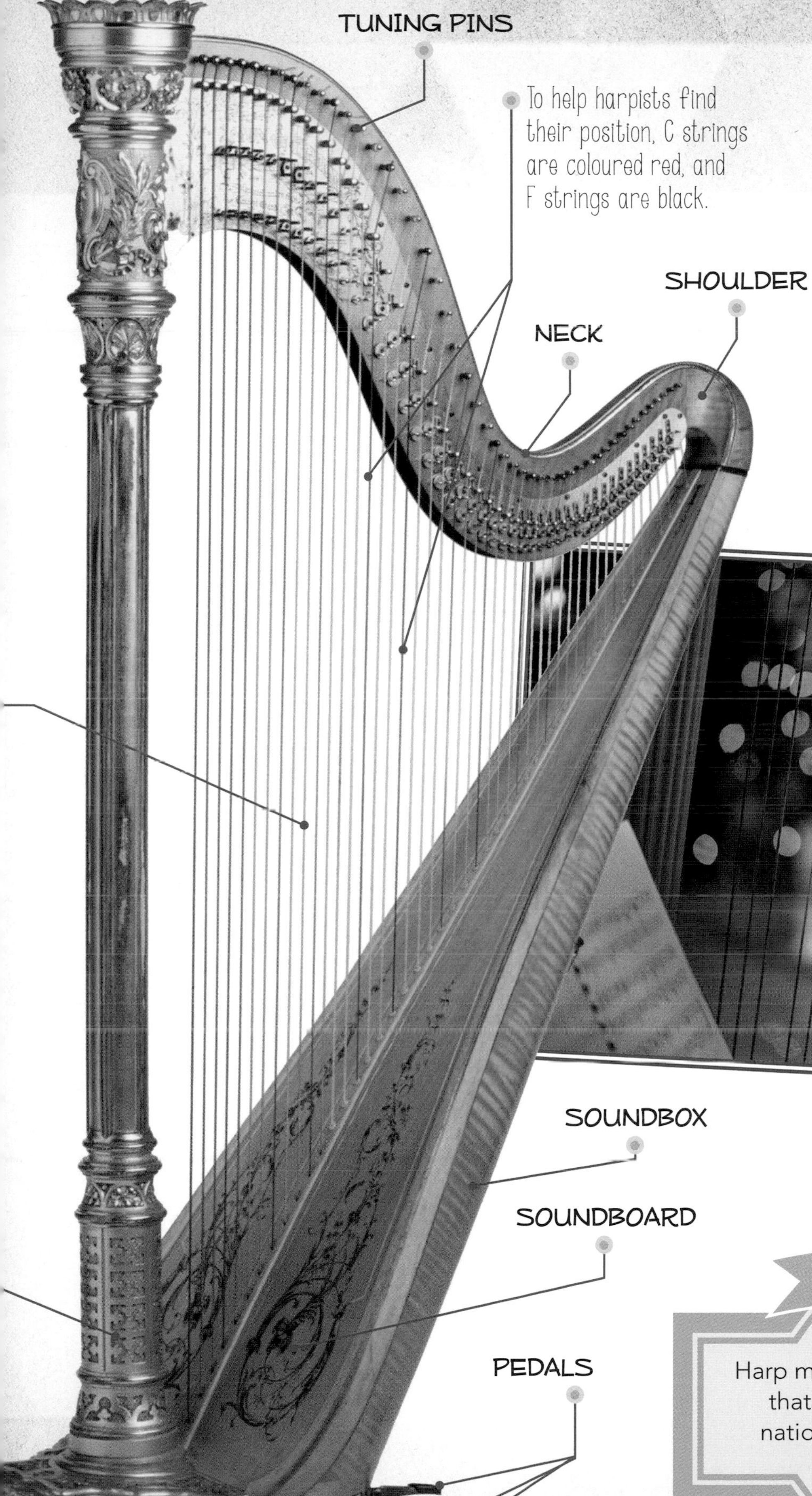

SOUNDBOX

TOP: A harpist plucks the strings of a modern harp.

SOUNDBOARD

PEDALS

DID YOU KNOW?

★

Harp music is so popular in Ireland that the harp is the country's national symbol, displayed on its coat of arms.

THE GUITAR

THE SIX-STRINGED ACOUSTIC GUITAR DIDN'T TAKE ITS CURRENT FORM UNTIL THE MID-19TH CENTURY. However, its ancestors, such as the lute and the harp, are among the oldest instruments in existence. And guitar-like instruments have been around since the Middle Ages. Because of its relatively quiet sound, the guitar is used in small ensembles, such as flamenco bands, or as a solo instrument, rather than in orchestras. Its much louder modern successor, the electric guitar, became perhaps the Western world's most popular instrument in the second half of the 20th century.

SUGGESTED LISTENING

Joaquín Rodrigo
Concierto de Aranjuez

Francisco Tárrega
Recuerdos de la Alhambra

Django Reinhardt
Appel Direct

INVENTING THE GUITAR

The word 'guitar' comes from the Latin 'cithara', a name for stringed instruments in around the 12th century, although these were more like lutes than modern guitars. The instrument that would eventually become the acoustic guitar was a Renaissance invention with strings arranged in four or five courses (pairs of identical notes, or the same note an octave apart). Instruments with six single strings appeared in the 1700s, and the instrument reached its final modern form in around 1850.

RIGHT: A modern six-string acoustic guitar.

MAKING A GUITAR

First, individual pieces for the front, back, ribs and neck are carved. The ribs are softened in boiling water, shaped, and then the body is glued together. A fingerboard with metal frets is glued to the neck, along with the tuning heads. A metal rod is inserted into the neck and body to help the instrument cope with the tension of the strings. Once the neck and body have been stuck together, the bridge, nut, saddle and strings are finally added.

BELOW: Making guitars in a modern-day workshop.

ABOVE: A boy learns to play the guitar.

PLAYING THE GUITAR

A right-handed player uses the fingers of their left hand to press down the strings to form notes (if just one string is pressed) and chords (if more than one string is pressed). Their right hand picks out the notes or strums the chords either using their fingers or a pick held between the thumb and first finger (some picks are worn over the thumb and fingertips). For left-handed players, the left- and right-hand roles are reversed.

DID YOU KNOW?

The first electric guitars were invented in the 1930s. They convert the strings' vibrations into electrical signals, which can then be loudly amplified.

HEADSTOCK
Where the tuning heads sit.

TUNING (MACHINE) HEADS
Turned to alter the pitch of the strings.

NECK
The head and neck are made from a single piece of wood.

NUT
Hard piece of plastic with six grooves for spacing the strings.

FINGERBOARD
Usually made of rosewood or ebony.

FRETS
To mark the position of the notes - in semitones - along the neck.

BODY
Acoustic guitars are usually made of spruce or cedar - strong lightweight woods that vibrate easily.

RIB

ROSETTE
Decoration.

SOUND HOLE

STRINGS
Usually made of either nylon or steel - tuned, from lowest to highest, to E, A, D, G, B, E.

SADDLE
Plastic piece for spacing strings.

BRIDGE

67

WIND
INSTRUMENTS

WIND INSTRUMENTS COME IN ALL SHAPES AND SIZES AND FROM ALL OVER THE WORLD. However, they all make their sounds in the same way – from the movement of air. For most, the air is provided by the breath of the player. However, some, such as the concertina and bagpipes, use hand-powered bellows.

ORCHESTRAL WIND INSTRUMENTS

ABOVE: The wind section of an orchestra playing together.

In a standard orchestra, the wind instruments are the piccolo, flute, oboe, clarinet and bassoon. All were once made of wood – which is why they're also known as woodwind instruments. Modern flutes and piccolos are constructed almost entirely of metal and all the orchestral wind instruments have metal parts. The wind section sits just behind the string section.

FLUTE (see pages 70–71)
FROM: Germany
INVENTED: 19th century (modern flute)
The standard concert flute is pitched in the key of C and has a range of three octaves. There are other types of flute that play in lower ranges, including the G alto flute and low C bass flute, but these rarely feature in orchestras.

PICCOLO
FROM: Europe
INVENTED: 18th century
Half the size of the concert flute, the piccolo plays the highest notes in the whole orchestra – an octave higher than the flute. Some large orchestras have dedicated piccolo players, but in smaller orchestras, one of the flute players usually doubles up.

CLARINET (see pages 72–73)
FROM: Germany
INVENTED: 18th century
There are usually four clarinets in an orchestra – an E flat, two B flats and a bass clarinet. It's the only orchestral wind instrument with a single **reed**.

OBOE

FROM: France

INVENTED: 17th century

Although it looks a bit like a clarinet, the oboe is played using a double reed – two thin pieces of wood fastened together. The oboist (oboe player) blows these reeds, causing them to vibrate, which creates the sound. Unlike the clarinet, which is mainly cylindrical, the oboe is shaped like a cone. An orchestra has between two and four oboes.

BASSOON

FROM: France

INVENTED: 17th century

The bassoon plays the lowest notes in the wind section. Its relative, the contrabassoon, can play the lowest notes in the entire orchestra, although it's used much less frequently. The standard bassoon consists of around 2.4 metres (8 feet) of wood and metal tubing bent into a U shape. Like the oboe, it's played using a double reed. An orchestra has between two and four bassoons.

OTHER WIND INSTRUMENTS

Bagpipes
FROM: Middle East
INVENTED: c. 500BCE

Panpipes
FROM: Greece
INVENTED: c. 2000BCE

Piano accordion
FROM: Europe
(France and Germany)
INVENTED: 19th century

Recorder
FROM: Europe
INVENTED: c. 14th century

Harmonica
FROM: Germany
INVENTED: 19th century

Saxophone
FROM: Belgium
INVENTED: 1840

THE FLUTE

THE FLUTE IS THE SECOND SMALLEST AND SECOND HIGHEST SOUNDING INSTRUMENT IN THE WIND FAMILY, AFTER THE PICCOLO. It has a bright, clear sound, and can be used to produce high, piercing notes or soft, breathy ones. The flute's sound is made by blowing air into the instrument. The flautist (flute player) doesn't blow into a mouthpiece, but over the top of a hole – a bit like how you blow over the top of a bottle to make a noise. The flautist changes notes by pressing down keys to cover the instrument's holes.

MAKING A FLUTE

The flute is a long metal cylinder divided into three sections: the headjoint, the body and the footjoint. These can be taken apart to make the flute easier to store. The instrument's body, holes and keys are crafted out of the same type of metal, usually silver (or silver-plated nickel), although other metals are sometimes used, including platinum and gold.

KEYS
The keys are pressed down to cover the holes, forming the notes.

ROD SYSTEM
The keys sit above the body on a system of thin rods, held in place by springs.

FOOTJOINT

BELOW: A traditional Serbian double flute carved from a single piece of wood.

INVENTING THE FLUTE

Flutes have been around for thousands of years, although it wasn't until around 1200 that the first side-blown (or transverse) flutes emerged. These wooden instruments grew in complexity over the next few centuries. In 1847, the German musician Theobald Boehm invented a new type of flute, using metal instead of wood, with a special fingering system that made it easier to play. It became the model for all modern flutes.

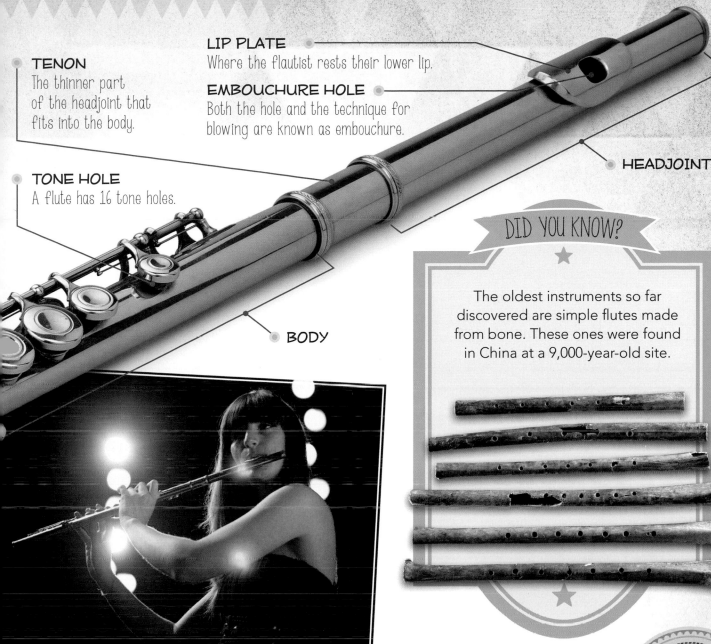

TENON
The thinner part of the headjoint that fits into the body.

LIP PLATE
Where the flautist rests their lower lip.

EMBOUCHURE HOLE
Both the hole and the technique for blowing are known as embouchure.

HEADJOINT

TONE HOLE
A flute has 16 tone holes.

BODY

DID YOU KNOW?

The oldest instruments so far discovered are simple flutes made from bone. These ones were found in China at a 9,000-year-old site.

ABOVE: A flautist plays live on stage.

PLAYING THE FLUTE

With the flute held horizontally in front of the face, and their lower lip resting on the lip plate, the flautist blows a stream of air across the embouchure hole. Their fingers press down the keys, covering the holes, to change notes. By changing the way they blow – blowing harder or softer, or changing the angle of their lips – the flautist can produce a range of different sounds and tones.

SUGGESTED LISTENING

James Galway
Annie's Song

Johann Sebastian Bach
Flute Suite in D minor

Claude Debussy
Syrinx

THE CLARINET

COMMONLY USED IN BOTH CLASSICAL MUSIC AND JAZZ, THE CLARINET IS NOT A SINGLE INSTRUMENT BUT A WHOLE FAMILY. There are more than a dozen types, ranging from the high-pitched piccolo clarinet to the low contrabass clarinet. The B flat soprano clarinet is the most popular, with a range of more than four octaves – the widest of any wind instrument. Symphony orchestras usually have four clarinets – an E flat, two B flats and a bass clarinet. A clarinet player is known as a clarinettist.

ABOVE: Chalumeaux from the Baroque and Classical eras.

INVENTING THE CLARINET

Invented in the early 18th century by the German instrument maker Johann Christoph Denner, the clarinet was based on an instrument called the chalumeau. The chalumeau was played with a reed and had a range of just one octave. Denner added keys, allowing it to play a wider range of notes. Further improvements were made in the 1800s with a new fingering system based on Theobald Boehm's fingering system for the flute.

REED
The clarinet is the only instrument in the orchestra that uses a single reed.

LIGATURE
Metal device that holds the reed in place on the mouthpiece. It's tightened with a screw.

MOUTHPIECE

BARREL
Unlike other wind instruments, the clarinet is the same width all the way down until it flares out into a bell.

UPPER SECTION

MAKING A CLARINET

Clarinets are usually made of a dark-coloured wood called granadilla, although plastic, rubber and metal are also sometimes used. The instrument maker carves a single block of wood into a long cylinder, bores a hole down the centre, drills seven tone holes, and then adds 17 metal keys (usually silver-plated nickel). The reed is made from cane – a type of tough grass – or sometimes a synthetic material.

ABOVE: A clarinet maker works in his studio.

ABOVE: Four clarinettists playing as part of an orchestra.

SUGGESTED LISTENING

George Gershwin
Rhapsody in Blue

Mozart
Clarinet Concerto in A

Acker Bilk
Stranger on the Shore

PLAYING THE CLARINET

The clarinettist plays the instrument by blowing air through the mouthpiece and over the reed, causing it to vibrate. This vibration creates the sound which travels through the instrument's body and out through the tone holes and **bell**. To change notes, the clarinettist places their fingers over the tone holes or presses down combinations of keys.

DID YOU KNOW?

The biggest clarinet, the contrabass, is 2.7 m (9 ft) long.

TONE HOLES

KEYS
When pressed, the keys move pads down to cover the tone holes, forming notes.

LOWER SECTION
The body is split into five sections so it can be easily stored.

BELL

73

BRASS
INSTRUMENTS

STRANGE AS IT MAY SEEM, BRASS INSTRUMENTS ARE NOT CATEGORIZED BY WHETHER THEY ARE MADE OF BRASS (ALTHOUGH MOST ARE), BUT BY HOW THEIR SOUNDS ARE MADE.

To qualify as a brass instrument, the player must vibrate – or buzz – their lips against the mouthpiece to produce sounds. This means that some wooden instruments, such as the didgeridoo, are brass instruments, while some reed instruments made of brass, such as the saxophone, are wind instruments.

ABOVE: French horns, trumpets, trombones and a tuba play together in the brass section of an orchestra.

ORCHESTRAL BRASS INSTRUMENTS

There are four brass instruments in a standard orchestra: the trumpet, trombone, French horn and tuba. As they are the loudest instruments in the orchestra, they are usually placed behind the wind section, so that they don't overwhelm the other, quieter instruments.

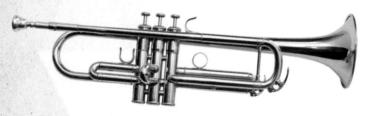

TRUMPET (see pages 76–77)
FROM: Germany (valve trumpet)
INVENTED: 19th century
Trumpets made of animal horns, conch shells, wood and metal have been around for thousands of years. The trumpets used in orchestras have valves (or buttons) for changing notes and were invented in the early 19th century. These are usually pitched in the key of C, although the smaller, higher-sounding B flat piccolo trumpet is also sometimes used. An orchestra has between two and four trumpets.

TROMBONE (see pages 78–79)
FROM: Europe
INVENTED: 15th century
Unlike the other instruments in the brass section, which use valves, the trombone is played using a slide, which gives it its distinctive swooping sound. There are usually three trombones in an orchestra.

FRENCH HORN

FROM: Germany

INVENTED: 19th century

An adaptation of a 17th-century French hunting instrument, the French horn has a large bell and around 5 m (17 ft) of tubing curled into a circular shape. As well as changing notes using valves, the horn player can also affect the sound by placing their hand in the bell, which muffles the sound, or by pointing the bell upwards, which creates a louder tone. An orchestra usually has four French horns.

TUBA

FROM: Germany

INVENTED: 19th century

Made of 5.4 m (18 ft) of coiled metal tubing, the tuba is the largest, lowest-sounding and heaviest of the brass instruments. It's also one of the youngest, having been invented in the early 19th century. There is usually just one tuba in an orchestra, tuned to C or B flat.

OTHER BRASS INSTRUMENTS

Bugle

FROM: Germany

INVENTED: 18th century

Flugelhorn

FROM: Germany

INVENTED: 19th century

Cornet

FROM: France

INVENTED: 19th century

Serpent

FROM: France

INVENTED: 16th century

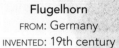

Didgeridoo

FROM: Australia

INVENTED: c. 500

Euphonium

FROM: Germany

INVENTED: 19th century

Sousaphone

FROM: United States

INVENTED: 19th century

THE TRUMPET

USED IN ORCHESTRAS AND AS A SOLO JAZZ INSTRUMENT, THE TRUMPET IS ONE OF THE SMALLEST MEMBERS OF THE BRASS FAMILY.

It can produce a variety of sounds from long, clear notes to piercing, angry stabs and quick jaunty melodies. There are many different types of trumpet, from the low-sounding bass trumpet to the high-sounding piccolo trumpet. The most common is the B flat trumpet, favoured by jazz musicians, although the smaller C trumpet usually features in orchestras because of its bright, lively tone.

RIGHT: An English hunting horn made of ivory from the 14th century.

VALVES
Pressing a valve increases the length of tube the air must pass through, lowering the note.

LITTLE FINGER HOOK

MOUTHPIECE

THUMB HOOK

SUGGESTED LISTENING

Wynton Marsalis
Flight of the Bumblebee
(by Nikolai Rimsky-Korsakov)

Henry Purcell
Trumpet Tune and Bell Symphony

Arturo Sandoval
Mambo Caliente

PLAYING THE TRUMPET

The trumpet player gets their instrument to make a sound by vibrating or 'buzzing' their lips against the mouthpiece. This sends a column of air into the trumpet, which is then amplified by the bell at the other end. To change notes, the player presses down different combinations of three valves, or buttons.

RIGHT: Playing a C note on a trumpet.

INVENTING THE TRUMPET

Simple trumpets made of animal horns, clay and, later, metal have been around since ancient times. However, these were 'natural' trumpets, like modern bugles, which didn't have valves. Instead, the player changed notes by changing how they blew. The modern valve trumpet was invented in 1818 by two German instrument makers, Friedrich Blühmel and Heinrich Stölzel. This vastly increased the amount of music a trumpet could play, making it a soloist's instrument.

ABOVE: Sealing the seam of a trumpet.

THIRD VALVE FINGER RING

BELL

TUNING SLIDE
Variations in temperature can make the trumpet go slightly out of tune. This can be corrected by moving the tuning slide to change the pitch.

WATER KEY
A valve for emptying liquid (in other words, saliva) that has collected inside the instrument. It's also known as the 'spit valve'.

MAKING A TRUMPET

The main part of a trumpet is a metal (usually brass) tube around 148 cm (58 in) long. It is bent twice to form a rounded oblong shape. The tube flares out into a bell shape at one end to project and amplify the sound. There are three (or sometimes four) piston valves set on springs – these are for changing notes. Players blow into a cup shaped mouthpiece.

DID YOU KNOW?
★

Trumpets are often used for military purposes. Here a trumpeter plays at the Changing the Guard ceremony at Buckingham Palace, London.

THE TROMBONE

INVENTED MORE THAN 500 YEARS AGO, THE TROMBONE IS ONE OF THE OLDEST MEMBERS OF THE BRASS FAMILY.

It's the only instrument to use a slide to change notes, giving it a distinct see-saw sound. Modern orchestras tend to feature three trombones – two tenors and one bass. The B flat tenor is the most commonly played version. It's pitched midway between the B flat trumpet and the B flat tuba. A trombone player is known as a trombonist.

ROTARY VALVE
Opens the coiled tubing attached to the bell.

TUNING SLIDE
For finely adjusting the instrument's pitch.

MOUTHPIECE
Detachable and similar in shape to a trumpet's.

1ST SLIDE BRACE (OR STRUT)
Where the player holds the trombone.

2ND SLIDE BRACE (OR STRUT)
The second brace is used to move the slider.

INVENTING THE TROMBONE

The first trombones were essentially trumpets with an added slide and were known as sackbuts. The name is believed to be a combination of the old French words *sacquer* ('to pull') and *boter* ('to push'). Although widely used in the Renaissance and Baroque periods, it wasn't until Romantic times that it became a fixture of the symphony orchestra. The design of the trombone has changed little over the centuries.

LEFT: A Baroque musician plays a sackbut, an early form of trombone.

MAKING A TROMBONE

Trombones are usually made out of brass. Skilled craftsmen shape the bell stem and flare, using hammers and lathes. Then they make the rest of the tubing, consisting of several separate sections. Each piece is filled with ice to stop it from buckling while they bend it into shape. Metal balls are pushed through the tubing to make sure it is the right diameter. The pieces are then soldered together.

ABOVE: A trombone maker at work in his studio.

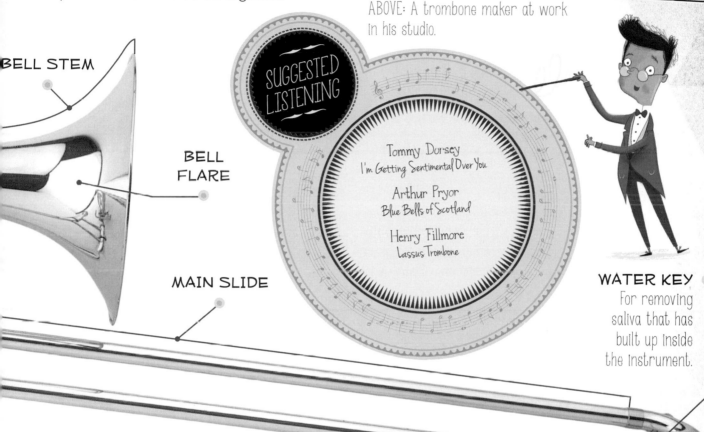

BELL STEM

BELL FLARE

MAIN SLIDE

WATER KEY
For removing saliva that has built up inside the instrument.

SUGGESTED LISTENING

Tommy Dorsey
I'm Getting Sentimental Over You

Arthur Pryor
Blue Bells of Scotland

Henry Fillmore
Lassus Trombone

PLAYING THE TROMBONE

Trombonists blow into their instrument in the same way as trumpet players, buzzing their lips against the mouthpiece. But unlike trumpet players, who press down valves to change notes, the trombonist uses a slide. The slide can be pulled backwards and forwards to any one of seven positions, altering the length of tubing, which shifts the pitch of the note.

RIGHT: Trombonist Raoul de Souza uses his slide to get the right sound.

PERCUSSION
INSTRUMENTS

BELOW: The percussion section of an orchestra contains a wide variety of instruments.

PERCUSSION INSTRUMENTS ARE MAINLY USED TO KEEP THE RHYTHM.
They also create drama and emphasize certain parts of the music. All percussion instruments are played by being either hit, shaken or scraped. Some percussion instruments, such as the xylophone, are tuned, while others, such as the bass drum, are not.

ORCHESTRAL PERCUSSION

This is the most varied section of the orchestra. Composers can use a range of instruments to add different effects and textures to their music. An orchestral percussionist is therefore expected to be able to play lots of instruments. Some of the most commonly used percussion instruments in an orchestra are the timpani, xylophone, cymbals, bass drum and snare drum. However, the specific instruments can vary greatly from piece to piece.

CYMBALS

FROM: Ottoman Empire (Turkey)
INVENTED: c. 17th century
Consisting of round, concave metal plates, cymbals are generally used to add excitement to a piece of music, rather than to keep the rhythm. There are many different types, ranging from tiny finger cymbals to large crash cymbals. They can be hit together or played with sticks, mallets or brushes.

ABOVE: A crash cymbal.

TIMPANI

FROM: Ottoman Empire (Turkey)
INVENTED: c. 15th century
Known for their big, booming, rolling beats, timpani are also known as kettle drums. Each drum consists of a copper bowl topped with a plastic drumhead, which is played using felt-tipped mallets. Unlike the snare, timpani are pitched to particular notes.

ABOVE: Timpani are played with felt-tipped mallets.

XYLOPHONE

FROM: South East Asia
INVENTED: c. 9th century
A cross between a set of woodblocks and a keyboard, the xylophone is a tuned percussion instrument. Orchestral versions have 42–48 wooden (or fibreglass) bars arranged like a piano keyboard, which are struck with mallets. The bars are connected to metal tubes which produce the instrument's bright, ringing sound.

LEFT: A xylophone with metal tubes called resonators hanging below tuned wooden bars.

SNARE DRUM

FROM: Switzerland
INVENTED: 15th century

The snare drum is made of a wooden cylinder with two plastic drum heads (skins) attached to the top and bottom. A set of wires known as a snare is fixed to the bottom head. This rattles when the drum is played, giving it its unique 'buzzing' sound.

LEFT: A snare drum is usually played with either wooden sticks or brushes.

BASS DRUM

FROM: Ottoman Empire (Turkey)
INVENTED: c. 17th century

Resembling a giant snare drum (but without the snare), the bass drum is the biggest drum in the orchestra. Its large, heavy sound is used to add mood and texture to a piece of music. Most drums have two heads.

BELOW: A bass drum with a mallet.

OTHER PERCUSSION INSTRUMENTS

Triangle
FROM: Europe
INVENTED: c. 13th century

Gong (Tam Tam)
FROM: China
INVENTED: c. 7th century BCE

Chimes (Tubular Bells)
FROM: France
INVENTED: 19th century

Glockenspiel
FROM: Europe
INVENTED: 18th century

Maracas
FROM: South America
INVENTED: c. 500BCE

Castanets
FROM: Middle East
INVENTED: c. 1000BCE

Tambourine
FROM: Middle East
INVENTED: c. 1000BCE

Congas
FROM: Cuba (via Africa)
INVENTED: 19th century

Bongos
FROM: Cuba
INVENTED: 19th century

Claves
FROM: Cuba
INVENTED: 19th century

Cabasa
FROM: South America (via Africa)
INVENTED: 19th century

Wood block
FROM: South America (via Africa)
INVENTED: 19th century

Whip
FROM: South America (via Africa)
INVENTED: 19th century

THE DRUM KIT

THE DRUM KIT ISN'T ONE INSTRUMENT SO MUCH AS SEVERAL.

A drum kit allows a single musician to play numerous percussion instruments at the same time, using drumsticks and foot pedals. The standard drum kit consists of a snare drum, bass drum, hi-hat, tom-toms and cymbals. Other instruments, such as wood blocks and cowbells, can also be added to the kit. Drum kits are widely used in jazz and popular music, whereas orchestras tend to utilize individual percussion instruments.

SUGGESTED LISTENING

Gene Krupa
Sing, Sing, Sing

Dave Brubeck
(Joe Morello)
Unsquare Dance

Buddy Rich
West Side Story Medley

INVENTING THE DRUM KIT

Until the late 19th century, all percussion instruments were played separately. Most orchestras employed several percussionists, but the lack of space in many theatres led to fewer percussionists tackling several instruments. Pedals for playing the bass drum (and later the hi-hat) were developed, as were pieces of apparatus to suspend drums and cymbals around the percussionist. By the 1930s, the drum kit had taken on its modern form.

BELOW: A 1920s kit with four wooden blocks and a tray of hand-held percussion instruments.

MAKING A DRUM

The drum shell (body) is made either from a single piece of wood, which is softened by steam and bent into shape, or built up layer by layer using thin pieces of wood. Brackets called lugs are added to the side and then plastic heads (skins) are pulled over the top and bottom. These are held in place by metal hoops. Tension rods are passed through holes in the hoops and into the lugs.

BELOW: Making a drum in a modern-day factory.

HI-HAT
Consists of two cymbals held face to face. It is played with sticks or a pedal that can clash the cymbals together.

SNARE DRUM
A ribbon of thin wires, known as a snare, sits against the bottom head, giving the drum its distinctive buzzing sound.

CRASH CYMBAL
Used for making loud crashes to highlight certain parts of the music.

MIDDLE TOM-TOM

HIGH TOM-TOM
A high-tuned drum.

RIDE CYMBAL
Used for keeping a steady 'riding' rhythm.

TENSION ROD
Can be tightened to tune the drum.

LUG

BASS DRUM
The lowest-sounding drum, often used for keeping the main beat.

PEDALS

FLOOR TOM-TOM
The lowest-sounding tom-tom.

PLAYING THE DRUM KIT

A drummer usually plays sitting on a stool, with a drumstick in each hand. Many employ a cross-arm technique where the right hand plays the hi-hat (for a right-handed player), while the left hand plays the snare. The right foot plays the kick drum using a pedal, while the left foot controls the hi-hat. All other drums are played using sticks.

RIGHT: The jazz drummer Buddy Rich in concert in 1973.

KEYBOARD INSTRUMENTS

THOUGH ALL KEYBOARD INSTRUMENTS LOOK VERY SIMILAR, THERE ARE GREAT DIFFERENCES IN HOW THEY MAKE THEIR SOUNDS.

Pianos, harpsichords and clavichords have strings, which are either struck or plucked. Pipe organs and harmoniums rely on air, while the sounds of the ondes Martenot and the synthesizer are the result of electronic trickery. However, all keyboard instruments are played in much the same way – by pressing down combinations of black and white keys.

ABOVE: A pianist is often positioned next to the strings in a classical orchestra.

RIGHT: Some harpsichords, like this one, had more than one keyboard.

ORCHESTRAL KEYBOARDS

There is no official keyboard section in a modern orchestra. Although the piano is widely used in classical music, it is not considered a fixed part of the orchestra. Instead, it is used as and when required, and situated to the side of the strings on the conductor's left. However, if it is the featured solo instrument in a concerto, it will be located at the front of the stage.

GRAND PIANO

(see pages 86–87)

FROM: Italy

INVENTED: 18th century

Classical musicians nearly always perform on grand pianos, which are regarded as having a rich, high-quality sound. A full-size concert grand piano can be 3 m (10 ft) long. The strings stretch horizontally from the keyboard towards the back of the piano. The hammers sit below the strings. After striking a note they fall back into position.

RIGHT: A grand piano.

HARPSICHORD

FROM: Italy

INVENTED: 15th century

The harpsichord was the most popular keyboard instrument of the 17th and 18th centuries. Indeed, at this time, the harpsichord player was regarded as the leader of the orchestra. Instead of being hit with hammers like a piano, the harpsichord's strings are plucked by plectrums (known as quills). This gives the instrument its clear, tinkly sound.

OTHER KEYBOARD INSTRUMENTS

UPRIGHT PIANO

FROM: Austria
INVENTED: late 18th century
With its vertical strings, the upright piano stands around 115 cm (45 in) tall.

CLAVICHORD

FROM: central Europe
INVENTED: 14th century
This is the earliest of the stringed keyboard instruments. The sounds are made by small metal blades striking the strings.

PIPE ORGAN

(see pages 88–89)
FROM: central Europe
INVENTED: c. 13th century
Owing to its huge size and immobility, the pipe organ is nearly always played as a solo instrument or accompanied by a choir.

HARMONIUM

FROM: France
INVENTED: 19th century
The harmonium works by blowing air – usually from foot-powered bellows – over a set of tuned brass reeds, and is widely used in Indian music.

ONDES MARTENOT

FROM: France
INVENTED: 1920s
Invented by the French cellist Maurice Martenot, the ondes Martenot was one of the first electronic instruments. It produces an eerie, wavering tone.

KEYBOARD SYNTHESIZER (see page 9)

FROM: United States
INVENTED: 1960s
This is an extremely versatile instrument whose sounds are created entirely electronically.

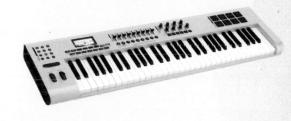

ELECTRIC ORGAN

FROM: United States
INVENTED: 1930s
The Hammond organ (below) was invented by the American engineer Laurens Hammond. It is one of the most popular electric organs, regularly featured in jazz and popular music.

THE PIANO

SINCE ITS INVENTION IN THE LATE 18TH CENTURY, THE PIANO HAS BECOME ONE OF THE WORLD'S MOST POPULAR INSTRUMENTS.

It is used today in everything from orchestral pieces to jazz and popular music. One of the piano's main attractions is its versatility. With 88 keys, it has a range of over seven octaves. Pianists (piano players) can play several notes simultaneously, allowing them to create complex chords. There are two main types of piano: the large grand piano and the smaller upright piano.

SUGGESTED LISTENING

Edvard Grieg
Piano Concerto in A minor

Beethoven
Fur Elise

Scott Joplin
The Entertainer

INVENTING THE PIANO

Invented by the Italian instrument maker Bartolomeo Cristofori (1655–1731), the piano was an improvement on two earlier keyboard instruments – the clavichord and the harpsichord. In a clavichord, the strings are hit with metal blades called tangents, while in a harpsichord they are plucked by quills. Pianos use felt-covered wooden hammers. This allows the instrument to be played both as loudly as a harpsichord and as quietly as a clavichord.

ABOVE: A clavichord.

RIGHT: A harpsichord.

MAKING A PIANO

Putting together a piano is a long, complicated process with many stages. The outer wooden rim – usually maple or beech – is put together first. Supporting braces are added and the soundboard – a piece of spruce – is carefully slotted into position. Next comes the cast iron frame (or plate), the strings and pin block, followed by the keys and hammers. Finally, the three legs and pedals are attached, and the piano is ready.

LEFT: An employee putting together a piano at the famous Steinway & Sons factory.

PIANO SIZE
A full-size concert grand piano can weigh 480 kg (990 lb).

STRINGS
Most pianos have 230 strings.

KEYBOARD
Modern keys are made of wood or plastic, rather than ebony and ivory as in previous centuries.

SOUNDBOARD
This is the surface that the strings vibrate against to make sound.

BELOW: The keyboard, frame, strings and tuning pins of a piano, from above.

PEDALS

DID YOU KNOW?
The piano's original name, pianoforte, means 'soft' (piano) 'loud' (forte) because of the range of volume it could produce.

PLAYING THE PIANO
The piano can be played with just one finger or all ten. When a pianist presses a key, a felt-covered hammer inside the piano strikes the relevant string. The vibrations are transmitted to the soundboard, which amplifies the sound. When the finger is taken off the key, the string is stopped from vibrating (silenced) by a damper. The harder the pianist presses, the louder the note. Three pedals can also be used to alter the instrument's sound.

THE PIPE ORGAN

THE PIPE ORGAN IS ONE OF THE WORLD'S OLDEST, LARGEST AND LOUDEST INSTRUMENTS.

It's like an enormous set of whistles, consisting of long metal pipes that play notes when air is pumped through them. These are controlled using a 61-key keyboard. As each pipe plays a different note, and each key operates a different pipe, there has to be a minimum of 61 pipes. However, most organs have several sets of pipes, known as ranks, which produce different sounds, each made of 61 pipes. Some of the largest organs have tens of thousands of pipes.

INVENTING THE PIPE ORGAN

The pipe organ's ancestor is the ancient Greek hydraulis, which used water pressure to force air through a series of pipes. By the Middle Ages, water had been replaced by hand- (or foot-) operated bellows, and the pipe organ had been adopted as a church instrument. Organs had also started to grow in size, as more pipes were added. Several enormous organs were constructed in the US in the early 20th century. Today, most organs rely on electrically powered bellows.

BELOW: Completed in 1890, the Sydney Town Hall Grand Organ is one of the largest in the world.

MAKING A PIPE ORGAN

Every organ is unique, as they are designed to fit their particular building. The main part of the organ is, of course, the pipes, which are usually made of metal or wood. There are two main types of organ pipe: the flue pipe, which looks and works a bit like a giant flute; and the reed pipe, which sounds notes when air makes a thin metal reed at the end of the pipe vibrate.

BELOW: The brass pipes of a reed organ.

ABOVE: The metal flue pipes of France's Narbonne Cathedral date back to 1739.

DID YOU KNOW?

The Boardwalk Hall Auditorium Organ, constructed in the early 1930s in Atlantic City, USA, is the largest and loudest musical instrument ever constructed, with 33,112 pipes and seven keyboards. Its loudest pipe can produce 130-decibel notes.

PIPES
The taller the pipe, the lower the note. Pipes range in length from a few centimetres to more than 15 m (60 ft).

SOUND
The very longest pipes have frequencies on the limit of what humans can hear.

WINDCHEST
Container of pressurized air beneath the pipes.

STOP KNOBS
These control the passage of air to the pipes.

SUGGESTED LISTENING

Felix Mendelssohn
Wedding March

Johann Sebastian Bach
Toccata and Fugue in D minor

Andrew Lloyd Webber
Phantom of the Opera

PLAYING A PIPE ORGAN

First, air is pumped into an airtight storage area called the windchest, which sits beneath the ranks of pipes. The keyboardist pulls out a stop knob, which moves a slider – a piece of wood with holes that line up with the bottom of one of the pipe ranks. When a key is pressed, a trap-door valve called a pallet flips down, allowing the pressurized air to pass from the windchest to a pipe, creating the sound.

BELOW: The keyboards and stop knobs of a pipe organ.

KEYBOARD
When not in use the keyboard is covered with a wooden lid.

PEDALS
Some of the keys are controlled by pedals.

THE CONDUCTOR

THE CONDUCTOR IS THE ONLY MEMBER OF THE ORCHESTRA WHO DOESN'T PLAY AN INSTRUMENT.

Instead, he or she stands at the front leading the musicians. At a basic level, this means getting them to start and finish at the same time. But it also involves setting the tempo and achieving the right sound balance – making sure no one is playing too loudly or too quietly. The conductor's role is to interpret the music and to get the musicians to play it the way he or she wants it to be played.

HOW TO CONDUCT

Conducting requires a lot of homework. Each musician has to learn only their part of a piece of music; but the conductor needs to know the entire score – when certain instruments come in, when they drop out and how everything is supposed to sound together. Some conductors have the score in front of them, while others conduct from memory.

LEFT: The noted British conductor Sir Thomas Beecham directing his orchestra in the 1930s.

HISTORY OF CONDUCTING

Before the early 19th century, orchestras didn't have conductors. It was the principal (or first) violinist who got the musicians to start together. However, as orchestra sizes increased, it became difficult for musicians on one side of the stage to hear those on the other. Initially, the conductor's role was just to keep the musicians playing at the same time. But as time went on, the role evolved and the conductor began to actively shape the orchestra's performance.

BELOW: Conductor and violinist Pinchas Zukerman leading the New York Philharmonic in 2012.

CUEING THE INSTRUMENTS

To make sure they can be seen by the musicians, the conductor stands on a raised platform (or podium). They may use a small pointed stick called a baton to count time and **cue** in the instruments, although some conductors use just their hands. Conductors spend a long time rehearsing with an orchestra to make sure the musicians play the music in the way they want.

LEFT: Sir Simon Rattle conducting the Berlin Philharmonic.

KEEPING TIME

Conductors set the tempo and keep the beat of the music by waving their batons in set patterns. This shows the musicians which time signature is being used. They also use other signals to affect the musicians' performance – for instance when they want a musician to play louder or softer, when they want a section to end sharply and when they want to change time signatures.

FAMOUS CONDUCTORS

Many noted composers and musicians became conductors in the 19th century, including Felix Mendelssohn (1809–1847) and Richard Wagner (1813–1883). In the 20th century, conducting became a specialized job. The best conductors were seen as performers in their own right. Some of the most celebrated include the Italian Arturo Toscanini (1867–1957), the German Herbert von Karajan (1908–1989) and the British Sir Thomas Beecham (1879–1961)

ABOVE: Toscanini using expressive gestures while leading a performance of the Vienna Philharmonic in 1937.

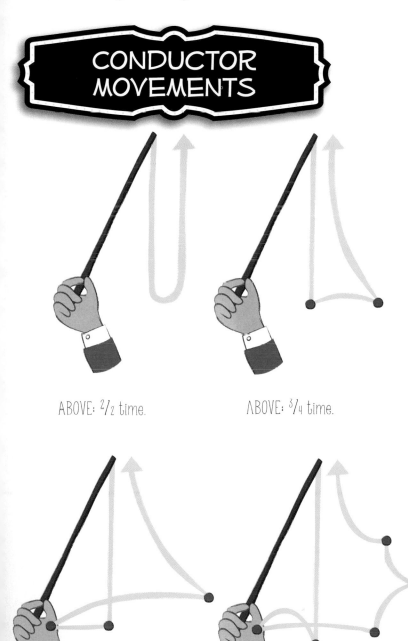

CONDUCTOR MOVEMENTS

ABOVE: $^2/_2$ time.

ABOVE: $^3/_4$ time.

ABOVE: $^4/_4$ time.

ABOVE: $^6/_8$ time.

DID YOU KNOW?

★

In the early days of conducting, before batons were widely used, conductors used whatever they had to hand to attract the musicians' attention, including rolled-up pieces of music and long wooden staffs.

THE YOUNG PERSON'S GUIDE TO THE ORCHESTRA

IN 1946, JUST AFTER THE SECOND WORLD WAR HAD ENDED, THE BRITISH COMPOSER BENJAMIN BRITTEN WROTE A PIECE OF MUSIC WITH THE AIM OF TEACHING CHILDREN HOW AN ORCHESTRA WORKS. *The Young Person's Guide to the Orchestra* (YPGO) introduces the audience to the instruments of the four main orchestral sections – wind, strings, brass and percussion – before showing how they all play together to make an orchestra.

ABOVE: Benjamin Britten with a group of students.

THE AIM

The piece was originally commissioned by the British Ministry of Education in 1946 to accompany an educational film called *Instruments of the Orchestra* which was to be shown in British schools. Its aim was to introduce children to the joy of music and instruments, and it has certainly inspired generations over the years.

THE PIECE

Based on the melody of a piece of music written by one of Britten's favourite composers, the London-born Henry Purcell (1659–95), the YPGO begins with the entire orchestra playing the main theme together. Then each section takes a turn playing the theme, beginning with the wind instruments, then the brass, then the strings and finally the percussion. Britten then features different instruments from each family in sections called variations.

LEFT: Portrait of the British composer Henry Purcell.

Wood Block
Castanets
Tambourine
Xylophone
Trombones
Triangle
Trumpets
Horns
Whip
Clarinets
Flutes
Piccolo
Harp
1st Violins
2nd Violins
Conduc

THE INSTRUMENTS AND THEIR VARIATIONS

Once all four sections have been introduced, individual instruments in each section are given some time in the spotlight to tackle a number of variations on the main theme. These variations highlight different dynamics in the music, with some instruments playing fast passages and others slow ones.

The variations are played in the following order:

WIND
Variation A: Piccolo and Flute
Variation B: Oboes
Variation C: Clarinets
Variation D: Bassoons

STRINGS
Variation E: Violins
Variation F: Violas
Variation G: Cellos
Variation H: Double Basses
Variation I: Harp

BRASS
Variation J: Horns
Variation K: Trumpets
Variation L: Trombones and Tubas

PERCUSSION
Variation M: Timpani, Bass Drum, Snare Drum, Gong (Tam Tam), Cymbals, Castanets, Wood Block, Tambourine, Triangle, Xylophone, Whip

nbals

Gong (Tam Tam)

Snare Drum

Bass Drum

Timpani

Tuba

Bassoons

Oboes

Double Bass

Violas

Cellos

ACTIVATE YOUR APP

Hold your device up to these pages!

Download your free app to explore and listen to the instruments featured in *The Young Person's Guide to the Orchestra*. Interact with each individual instrument and listen to it play. Then build your orchestra by placing each instrument in the correct section. Test your knowledge by trying the fun quiz – can you correctly identify the sounds? And finally listen to a full recital of *The Young Person's Guide to the Orchestra*.

GLOSSARY

ACOUSTIC
An acoustic instrument is one that amplifies its own sound without using electricity.

ALBUM
A collection of pre-recorded songs or pieces of music released as a single item for sale. Formats for albums have included vinyl records, magnetic tapes, CDs and, most recently, MP3s.

AMPLIFIED/AMPLIFIER
To amplify something is to increase its volume. An amplifier is a piece of equipment that increases the amplitude of an instrument's electrical signal to raise its volume.

ANALOGUE
A recording process in which sound is recorded as a continuous pattern onto magnetic tape.

ATONALITY
Atonal music does not follow standard harmonic relationships between notes, resulting in chords that can sound strange and unusual.

BALLAD
Traditionally, a ballad is a song that tells a story in a series of verses; more recently it has come to describe a type of slow, sentimental love song.

BASS
Bass notes are the lowest-sounding notes in a piece of music. Bass is also the name for the lowest vocal range.

BEAT
A beat is a moment of measured time used to divide up a song or a piece of music.

BELL
The flared end of a brass or wind instrument where the sound comes out.

CHORD
A group of three or more notes played at the same time.

CHORUS
The part of the song that is sung after each verse. It is usually designed to be catchy and memorable. A chorus can also be a large group of singers.

CHROMATIC SCALE
A group of 12 notes in a sequence of semitones. In Western music, the scale repeats after every 12th semitone (or 7th tone). See also Natural tones (page 65).

CLEF
A symbol at the start of a piece of musical notation informing the musician which notes the lines on the stave (see page 29) stand for.

CUE
A signal, either written in a piece of music or given as a gesture by the conductor, to indicate that a musician should start playing.

DIGITAL RECORDING
A recording process whereby sound information is converted into a series of numbers.

DISSONANCE
Music that does not follow usual harmonic rules and sounds harsh and discordant.

ELECTRIC
An electric instrument is one where the sounds are made by the instrument, but which are then converted into an electrical signal and greatly amplified.

ELECTRONIC
An electronic instrument is one where the sounds are created purely electronically by the instrument's technology.

ENSEMBLE
A group of musicians who play together.

FLAT
A semitone lower than a Natural tone (page 65). Flats and sharps are the black keys on a keyboard.

FREQUENCY
The number of times a repeated activity happens during a certain period of time.

HOOK
The catchy, memorable part of a song that is repeated throughout.

IMPROVISE
To make up music as it's being performed – musicians usually improvise around existing themes and tunes.

LOOP
A repeating section of a recorded piece of music.

MASTER RECORDING
The finished, approved version of a recording from which all other recordings are made.

MELODY
Notes that have been arranged into a distinctive pattern or sequence. Also known as a tune.

MODERNISM
Modernism was a style of music in the early 20th century that rejected many of the rules that had governed how music was written in previous centuries.

MOVEMENT
A self-contained section of a larger piece of music, such as a symphony.

MP3
A form of digital recording (see pages 34–35) in which those parts of the music that people don't normally hear (because they are too high or too low) are removed, so reducing the file size.

MULTITRACK
A recording technique in which different parts of a song are recorded separately and then mixed together to produce the final record.

MUSICAL NOTATION
Written symbols corresponding to the pitch, key, time signature and other features of a piece of music, which allow a musician to play a piece of music without having first heard it.

NATURAL TONES
In musical theory, musical notes are arranged in groups and given letter names: A, B, C, D, E, F and G. These are known as the seven natural tones and correspond to the white keys on a keyboard.

NEOCLASSICISM
A reaction against modernism, neoclassicism was a 20th-century style of music based on the traditional styles of previous centuries.

OCTAVE
A repeating pattern of 7 whole tones (or 12 semitones).

OFFBEAT
The unaccented or unstressed beats in a bar, such as the second and fourth beats in a standard bar of $^4/_4$ time. Some music, such as reggae, deliberately stresses the offbeats.

ORALLY
Things that are passed down orally are done so without anything being written down. Music that has been passed down orally has been learnt by ear.

OVERTURE
A one-movement piece of music that can be used to introduce an opera or can be performed separately.

PITCH
How high or low a note is – to alter the pitch is to make a note higher or lower.

PLAINCHANT
Also known as Gregorian chant, plainchant was a type of early European religious music, consisting of simple melodies sung in Latin, usually without harmonies or accompanying instruments.

REED
A piece of wood, cane or metal which is made to vibrate in some instruments so as to produce sound.

RHYTHM
The pulse or feel (rather than the notes) of music, made up of repeated percussive patterns.

SAMPLE
A small portion of music from one song that is copied and used to create another song. Recording music like this is known as sampling.

SCALE
A set of notes based on the pattern of intervals between the notes.

SEMITONE
The smallest musical interval used in most Western music, it is half of a whole tone.

SERIAL MUSIC
A type of 20th-century musical composition in which musicians use the 12 notes of the chromatic scale to create a pattern with each note featured once.

SHARP
A semitone higher than a Natural tone (page 65). Flats and sharps are the black keys on a keyboard.

SINGLE
A popular music song sold as an individual unit (or with another song) in a pre-recorded format. These formats have included vinyl records, magnetic tapes, CDs and, most recently, MP3s.

SOUND WAVE
A movement of air caused by a sound — this movement carries the sound to your ears where it is heard.

STAVE
In musical notation, a stave is a set of five horizontal lines representing different pitches on which musical notes are written.

STYLUS
A needle used for recording and playing records.

SYMPHONY
A large, instrumental work played by a full orchestra and usually consisting of three or four movements (parts).

SYNCOPATION
Changing the regular rhythm of a piece by emphasizing unusual or unexpected parts; stressing a beat that wouldn't normally be stressed.

TEMPO
The speed of a piece of music.

TIME SIGNATURE
A code, consisting of one number above the other written at the start of a piece. The bottom number tells the musician what length of beat is being used, while the top number tells them how many beats there are in each bar.

TREBLE
Treble notes are the highest-sounding parts in a piece of music.

WESTERN
Describes culture and music originating in Western Europe and the United States, also known as the West.

VINYL
A type of plastic used to make the majority of records sold between the 1950s and 1980s.

VIRTUOSO
A musician who displays a high level of skill at singing or playing a particular instrument.

INDEX